Memorandum to the African Americans

Preamble

There is a saying, "if you want to hide something from African Americans put it in a book." I hope this will not be the case, for "Memorandum to the African Americans." I dedicate this book to all African Americans, which have lived in America from 1619 until this day.

Introduction

I write this "Memorandum to the African Americans" through the Spirit of Hope, Faith, and Love; that has moved me all the days of my life. I'm an African American, descendent of slaves in America; I believe that I was destined to be a leader of African Americans. However, the years have caught up with me, yet my optimism, courage, and faith are still intact, to fight on to bring African Americans out of the dark prisons of poverty; let me tell you some of my history. I became the Chairman of the Black Foundation, and organization that I help founded after the riots in April (1992) in Los Angeles, California. When white police officers, were acquitted of the beating of Rodney King, an African-American. The beating was caught on video; Spike Lee shows it in his movie Malcom X.

After they were acquitted, a riot broke out, most of the black community was burn down. After South Central was burned down, which is a part of Los Angeles, there was a need for it to be rebuild. Before the riots, myself, Robert Bridges and Prentiss Jenkins, we were trying to put together the Black Fund. This Black Fund was organized to get funds in the hands of Blacks, to invest in their own businesses in the Black community. But after the riot, we turn our attention to, what the Black community would need to be rebuild. The term Rebuild L.A. was start by the Black Fund. We brainstorm and came up with Rebuild L.A., we print flyers about our effort to Rebuild LA… I must admit that Prentiss went out; post the flyer everywhere he could. He also reported that the national guard escorted him around South Central, allowing him to place the flyers everywhere he went.

The slogan Rebuild L.A. caught on and was adopt by Mayor Bradley, he made an organizing body call RLA, short for Rebuild L.A… We didn't get any credit for it, even though our flyers were all over L.A. and were shown often on the news. Before Mayor Bradley, came up with the organization RLA, many people including the news and politicians were continuingly calling the (Black Fund)

Memorandum to the African Americans

before we change the name to the Black Foundation, for information on how to rebuild L.A.

However, as construction began to increase, we change our focus from funding blacks, to rebuilding South Central. Robert and Prentiss began monitoring the sites, and the contractors that were starting to rebuild in the community. People were calling the number on the flyer to find out how they could get involved. At the time I was the spiritual leader, we all belong to Christ's Order, and I was also an employee of RLB Construction. As Robert and Prentiss began to monitor the sites, which were beginning to be rebuild in South Central. They began to notice that there were no blacks working on any of the sites. Also with further investigation, they found out that there were no black contractors, with contracts on the sites, throughout the black community. Robert and Prentiss came to me and said, as they often call me. Brother Saul! "there are no blacks on any of the construction sites that we have been monitoring."

They further pointed out that there wasn't even a Blackman doing security or even holding a water hose to keep the dust down on the sites, that were being graded. I was working on a project as a painter at the time for RLB construction. I was in disbelief; so I said, "I want to see these sites." They said, "we have twenty sites where you won't find not one black person working." I said to them, "I want to go and see if what you're saying is true." And I said, "if I find a black person is working on these sites, please don't bother me with this again," they agreed. We live together so we woke up that morning to go and see the sites, we got to the tenth site. I had enough; I was really beside myself when it began to sink in that what they were telling me was the truth.

Prentiss was keeping the numbers of everyone that called the Black Fund. I directed Prentiss to call all of them back; those that were construction workers or had a trade, to meet us at the first construction site, with their boots and tools, and be ready to go to other sites. We end up with 50 black men that morning that met with us. We took down their information, also what type of construction work they did, and we went from site to site. The only one that was to speak at the sites was me. The purpose for this was to keep from getting into an argument, but just to settle the issue of having no blacks working on the sites. We went to the sites and shut them down. I start out telling the supervisor that he is in violation, because there were no blacks on the site and that blacks have a right to work in their own community. I also point out that he didn't live in the community, he was taking

Memorandum to the African Americans

dollars out of the community, dollars that should stay in the community. I further point out that he purchased his food from outside the community, and he even purchased his gas outside the community. The site supervisors called the police, all the men with the Black Fund were instructed to stand quietly, orderly and to direct the police to speak to me, which they did. When they ask, "what was going on," I told them, "that the site was shut down because they had no blacks working on the site. This is discrimination where intentional or unintentional it is unacceptable; blacks have a right to work in their own community."

Most of the time the officers were black our Latinos that were sent out. They would ask, what authority do I have to do this? When they tried to get heavy handed, I would always point out. "If there weren't people like myself and the men standing with me, you wouldn't have a job in the police force." They thought about what I said, and knew it was true and every time they would back off. They would tell, the supervisor "he had to settle this in court" and they would leave, many of them shook my hand and confirmed I was telling the truth. They wouldn't have their job if it wasn't for someone like the Black Fund standing up for minorities.

I would then instruct the supervisor that he will have to call the general contractor and subcontractors. Let them know that they are going to have to hire black workers and contractors for their site, if they want to continue working in the community. I would point out to the general contractors and subcontractors. After you have built this site, blacks will be supporting the business while you have moved on. Taking the money, you were paid to another community, this is unacceptable. You have come into the community, and have taken the money, and Blacks didn't participate in the building of the community? Subsequently, with this spiel, they seem to get the message and began to comply with our wishes. The Black Fund began to grow by leaps and bounds. We end up being thought of as rebels; Mayor Bradley didn't like what we were doing. Also, city council members didn't like what we were doing, to help the community, but the community loved it.

One day as we were working to make sure blacks were on sites and getting contracts. We ran into Danny Bakewell of the Brotherhood Crusade; he is well known in the community. The Black Fund had it out with him because he stop's a job, where we were already negotiating with the general contractor. He had the community leaders with him; After a big blowout with Danny Bakewell, we retain the site. Later he informed us that the name the Black Fund was a name that he had

Memorandum to the African Americans

already secure. He had the name before we used it, and he wanted us to stop using it because he was getting calls that we work for him. The Black Fund, want to fight it out with him. I said, "I didn't want us to fight with him, because that is exactly what white people want, so they can say, "blacks always fight among themselves.""

I persuade the group that we should just change the name, and God will give us the name we need. The Black Fund had board members that resigned because I refused to fight with Danny Bakewell, he also set in motion to sue us. We had a brainstorming meeting to select a new name, so the Black Foundation was founded. I was elected to be the Chairman; we continue business as usual in this name (The Black Foundation). There were many people that got jobs and contracts, because of the efforts of the Black Foundation.

We receive letters from politicians thanking the Black Foundation, for the work we were doing in the community. We also held community unity meetings, a lot of the meetings were held at the Elegant Manor, with the help of Momma Moody. As we grew we needed more space so we move to the Ebony Showcase with Nick Stewart, who once played, "Lighting" on "Amos & Andy show." There was also Percy Pinkney, he is our Godfather in politics, we look to him for guidance in matters of politics. He works with BAPAC, a Black political organization to help elect black politicians. He also worked in Senator Dianne Feinstein office, his help and guidance were invaluable.

Lawyers from Irell & Manella put together the Black Foundation nonprofit status for free in 1993. I really wasn't happy with this, I wanted the Black Foundation to sell stock or change our name so we could sell stock, however, the Board wanted to go this route. I will always continue to promote, what African Americans should be doing, and that is producing businesses for profit, sharing this profit with each other, so we can change our circumstances. As I tried to let the Board know, we start out with the Black Fund to help black businesses; non-profit this isn't the road to go down, we shouldn't be trying to get money through a non-profit method. I wanted to use a new strategy so that African Americans could develop wealth among ourselves.

Something I believe even until today, when I brought this to the Board attention that African Americans had more than 282 billion dollars in spending power, at that time. I try to make the Board see what we should be doing; it was to no avail. Today African Americans have a trillion dollars in purchasing power. As I write this "Memorandum to the African Americans," we must learn to invest in

Memorandum to the African Americans

ourselves by becoming stockholders and capitalists, receiving dividends to promote passive income for African Americans. We need our money to work for us, rather than just working for our money. Also, that are money should be cycled and recycle among us several times before leaving our community. This is something I explain to the Board; it didn't go over very well. I will be discussing this in more detail in this message. I wanted to stop begging the white man for his help and stop looking to the white man for handouts. But the Board was happy with the direction that the Black Foundation was going in. We were obtaining multi-Million dollars' contracts for black and white contractors working together in the community, plus thousands of jobs for community residents.

We were invited to all type of events, as well as producing all type of events. Martin Luther King said, "I have a dream, that one day my four little children will live in a nation, where they will not be judge by the color of their skin, but by the content of their character." I have a revelation, that one day African Americans will realize that we must unite economically, leaving or rebuilding the ghetto plantations and stop picking consumer cotton, in other words stop being consumers slaves.

If we develop the wealth within our grasp, we will be accepted globally, and we will have the wealth to show our resolve. I have introduced myself for this purpose, that those who read this book will know, where I'm coming from, and where I'm headed too. I feel it is important to write this "Memorandum to the African Americans." My hope is that we as people will make our own promise land through loving, respecting and honoring each other, and uniting with one another economically and becoming shareholders and capitalists.

Yes, I will sell this book for a profit, because I'm a capitalist. I want to tell anyone that purchasing this book. I will use these monies to work to unite African Americans and raise them up; economically from the dead, for which they are deaf, dumb and blind to capitalism. They are self-trap for trying to fit in a white world, without developing wealth among our people. With the monies I will seek to break the chains of the lack of education, among African Americans, this education must be gear toward capitalism and technology. It would have to be a lot of money in the billions to make the revelation and vision have a chance at working.

I have an Associate degree in Software Development with a 3.95 GPA I'm also a member of National Technical Honor Society. I want young African Americans to understand how important it is to have a scientific education in

Memorandum to the African Americans

technology. We now live in the technological age, we no longer live in the industrial age, in which most of our mother, fathers and grandparents grew up in. Young African Americans need more than just a street or a public school education. Young African Americans must also be willing to put in the studying; need to get good grades and understand the technology that is constantly changing. As you read this book I will point out many things, that have kept African Americans from enjoying the wealth of this country. And how so many others have come to this country and become wealthy, while African Americans have continued to live in poverty.

It is commonly known that the prisons of America; are fill with African American men. African American men who have been caught up in the judicial system for crimes, they believe they wouldn't get caught doing. Such as using drugs, selling drugs and gang activity. Believing the way to get ahead in America is to break the law, not understanding the laws have been set up, to trap African American men and women. I will further discuss this in the book, in a manner that put this in perspective, for the purpose of getting a better understanding, about this trap.

My hope is to bring about an economic revolution; I have no illusion on how very difficult this will be. I now have experience and education to pursue this economic revolution. I believe there are millions of African Americans, that will be willing to participate in an economic revolution. But there must be leadership and the removal of the fear of each other in economic matters. The suspicion and disrespect of each other for wanting to develop wealth must be put aside.

African Americans will need to realize that a monetary sacrifice has to be made and that there is a financial risk involve in developing wealth. But there are also great rewards for those that work to propel this economic revolution. I am writing the brutal truth, African Americans as a group of people should have great wealth, but because of the lack of economic unity we suffer poverty. There should be no African Americans living on ghetto plantations, picking consumer cotton in America.

At the time of this writing, African Americans have a trillion dollars' in purchasing power. Without proper organizational leadership and economic unity, we will always be no more than consumer slaves, and will continue to live in poverty. Serving the country as our ancestors did when they were slaves on the plantation. Our purchasing power is helping immigrants, that have come to this

Memorandum to the African Americans

country illegally, and their families are enjoying the wealth of this country. Because of our lack of unity and economical respect for one another to develop the African American markets and culture. These immigrants have moved into the African American communities and sop up African-American purchasing power. Opening businesses in the African American communities, then turn around and move into the white communities. And the most important factor, that has been covering up, the white man allowed millions of immigrants to come into this country. When George Bush Jr. was President, African Americans didn't want to take minimal jobs for slave wages, they wanted higher pay.

He allowed millions of immigrants to come in this country to be used for cheap labor. Now their jobs are being sent out of the country because immigrants want higher pay. These immigrants now overrun the public schools and government services, African American children have the difficulty of going to school. Because of institutionalized racism and discrimination from white people and immigrants, which I will discuss later. Please continue to read "Memorandum to the African American." Where I discuss many things I have touched upon in this introduction. I dedicate this Introduction to all the African American leaders, that have gone on before me, they have at least start the path to economic freedom. Which I intend on completing with the help of God Almighty and African Americans.

First Printing: 2016

LULU Press Inc.

3101 HILLSBOROUGH ST.

RALEIGH, NC 27607

www.africanamericanorg.com

Memorandum to the African Americans

Table of Contents

Memorandum to the African Americans

The History

I want to speak briefly about the history of the African Americans, it is a history of human rights violations in America. The first thing an African American needs to know is that the history of America. Also, most of the world history has been white wash; meaning that white people have told the stories, and wrote the books and develop the entertainment of the world from a white perspective. This has given them an advantage in controlling the subconscious mind of African American children. When you are growing up seeing mostly white people on TV and in an advertisement it affects you.

There was a time when African Americans if they saw themselves on TV, advertisement or entertainment in the early days of TV they would be in a subservient part. As a child, you don't understand why white people have it better than African Americans, in a nation that teaches freedom, justice, and equality for all. Living in a nation that calls you names like "nigger, spook, spade and boy" to hurt your mentality. As a child, you wonder why white people hate you and want to hurt you when all you want to do is be an American, and be treat the same as a white American. Many African American leaders and white Americans, rose up to change these circumstances in America, to bring about the words of the Constitution, "That all men are created equal."

Looking back at this history, it will be more of a psychological assessment. White people are also called Caucasians, they are from the north part of the earth, from Russian, Europe and mix with the blood of Neanderthal, a people that are extinct, they had a lot of animal instincts with the desire to kill, this was pass on to the European homo sapiens. In this part of the world it gets very cold, they learn to kill animals and use their fur to keep them warm. They lived in caves before they began to develop their civilization, building wood and stone buildings, I believe because of the cold weather.

They learn to live together and work together to stay alive, as their history develop it progressed to royalty and the peasant, also known as the feudal system. The feudal system became the dominant system in Europe, which exist today call the rich and the poor, with the underlying foundation of capitalism. White people are rich and most African Americans are poor. White people desire to be rich and are willing to do what it takes to be rich. They are willing to take risks even if it means they could die to try to get rich. They're willing to travel the oceans in

Memorandum to the African Americans

order to find the riches of the world. There is a driving spirit in white people to control and master the elements of the earth and the people of earth, this is where capitalism started with white Europeans, and it is in full force today.

Many White people believe in inventing or stealing inventions. The gun was invented by the Chinese along with the gunpowder. When the Europeans got hold of this knowledge, they took warfare and conquering to a new level. With this new instrument (the gun) they have traveled the world. Killing and pillaging the world of goods and people. The Europeans travel to North America with the gun, and robbed the native Indians of their land, treasures, their lives and kill the buffalo for sport, to rob the Indians of their food and livelihood, they also brought diseases upon them.

White people are the master of the gun and the master of death. If you look at the movies, or television they are fill with this formula, stealing, murder, sex, money, violent, anger, hate, subliminal racism and a beautiful woman surrounded by drama. This formula is to evoke the emotions of the viewer. Also, most everything they sell; they use a beautiful white woman. Many African American men, when I was growing up want a white woman, because that's all they saw on TV and in an advertisement.

White people have learned and cultivate advertising techniques to an intoxicating level. This is how white people manipulate people, the terminology is marketing. In the 1600's white men stole and brought Africans from Africa, to build up America, by making them into slaves. The majority of work for America, came from this stock of Africans and from these Africans, which are the strongest people that ever lived on the earth, and from these Africans, emerge African Americans. Slavery has had a deep and devastating effect on African Americans even unto this day, the wounds and the scars can be seen.

Look back at Africans, they live on a continent that has weather, where it doesn't snow, the weather is hot. Africans didn't need coats, so killing animals for their fur to keep them warm wasn't needed. Africans have plenty of hunting ground in the jungle. They didn't wear a lot of clothing. They live in villages, where they built huts and were content with their living arrangements; meaning that they weren't trying to leave Africa in search of riches or a better life. They had wars and problems, but their interest wasn't to find riches because the land of Africa is very rich. The rich plant and animal life, affords them to live a comfortable life. Rooted in deep mystical rituals and eccentric traditions.

Memorandum to the African Americans

Egypt is in the land of Africa, noted for building the first civilization. When you look at movies and television the ruling people are white, that is why I pointed out that white people have white wash history. The three-thousand-year history of Egypt and the Pharaohs were all black. But the white wash history of the American movies and television would have you believe they were white. White Europeans set out to dominate the world, Caucasians Europeans traveling across the oceans; these Europeans are of England, Italy, Germany, France, Spain and Greece, there are more, that I haven't mentioned. Europeans traveling to all the continents of the earth, seeking treasure and world domination. Which they accomplish until 1960 when all nations wanted white Europeans to relinquish their hold on power in nations across the globe.

In the 1960's Africans Americans received civil rights and the rights to vote. We had great leaders that rose up in the sixties and most were assassinated, expect for the Honorable Elijah Muhammad of the Nation of Islam, he had sense enough to have the Fruit of Islam, his security to protect him. I believe that J Edgar Hoover head of the FBI had all of them assassinated, he always feared the rise of the Black Messiah. A leader that would raise the Blackman out of poverty into mainstream America.

J Edgar Hoover was an expert in hiding his hand, which I believe was full of murder. He hides the fact that he was a cross dress and a homosexual, until the day he died, so he was great in hiding, he had a great deal of Americans assassinated. Medgar Evers, one the first civil right leaders integrated University of Mississippi, John F. Kennedy embraced Martin Luther King Jr., Malcom X is new name Hajj Malik el-Shabazz, he was going before the United Nations to speak about the humans' rights violations perpetrated on African Americans by American.

Malcom X, (Mr. el-Shabazz) was going on that global stage to speak. J Edgar Hoover knew he had to stop Malcom X from speaking at the United Nations about the human rights violations on African Americans by America. If Malcom X was allowed to speak, it would make America look bad and take away their power to speak against other nations with human right violations, and it would show the hypocrisy of freedom, justice and equality in America.

Martin Luther King Jr., they felt that it was just a manner of time before he could actually be the first Black President, the CIA was order to kill him with the cover of the FBI. Bobby Kennedy could have help African Americans, but he was assassinated; because of the fear from politics of the middle east and possibly the

Memorandum to the African Americans

Mafia. Fred Hampton of the Black Panthers was feared because of his ability to unite black and white people. A black FBI agent was sent to info trait the Black Panthers so that Chicago Metro police could assassinate him while he slept. J. Edgar Hoover died shortly after Fred Hampton. The order to put African American leaders to death stop with the death of Fred Hampton, so far; after the death J. Edgar Hoover.

The Leadership for African Americas has always pointed toward protest and demonstration. African Americans have fought in all the wars of America, and white officials have always turned their back on African Americans, even though they fought with valor and distinction. I will not cover the whole history of African Americans or White Europeans. The history has been well documented, what I want to point out is the development of our nature. And how we as a people of earth have responded to the many trials that have been placed on African Americans. And why we react the way we do to situations that we have to end up in. As I continue to write this "Memorandum to the African Americans" it is important to touch upon our history. This why many African Americans are still poor and trap in the prison of poverty. Whitewash history has cause disenchantment, misdirection, disfranchisement, and falsehood. It now time to write about the problem.

Memorandum to the African Americans

The Problem

Willie Lynch wrote a letter to White slave owners that were having troubles with slaves back in 1712, this information is being used today and is affecting African Americans today. There are those that believe the letter is a hoax; However, the truth about dealing with slaves is in this letter. *Here is a portion of the letter, it says:*

Gentlemen, you know what your problems are; I do not need to elaborate. I am not here to enumerate your problems; I am here to introduce you to a method of solving them. In my bag here, I have a foolproof method for controlling your black slaves. I guarantee every one of you that if installed correctly it will control the slaves for at least 300 years. My method is simple. Any member of your family or your overseer can use it. I have outlined a number of differences among the slaves and make the differences bigger. **I use fear, distrust and envy for control.**

These methods have worked on my modest plantation in the West Indies and it will work throughout the South. Take this simple little list of differences and think about them. On top of my list is "age" but it's there only because it starts with an

"A." The second is "COLOR" or shade, there is intelligence, size, sex, size of plantations and status on plantations, attitude of owners, whether the slaves live in the valley, on a hill, East, West, North, South, have fine hair, course hair, or is tall or short. Now that you have a list of differences, I shall give you an outline of action, but before that, I shall assure you that distrust is stronger than trust and envy stronger than adulation, respect or admiration. The Black slaves after receiving this indoctrination shall carry on and will become self-refueling and self-generating for hundreds of years, maybe thousands. **Don't forget you must pitch the old black Male vs. the young black Male, and the young black Male against the old black male. You must use the dark skin slaves vs. the light skin slaves, and the light skin slaves vs. the dark skin slaves. You must use the female vs. the male. And the male vs. the female.** You must also have your white servants and overseers distrust all Blacks. **It is necessary that your slaves trust and depend on us. They must love, respect and trust only us.** Gentlemen, these kits are your keys to control. Use them. Have your wives and children use them, never miss an opportunity. **If used intensely for one year, the**

Memorandum to the African Americans

slaves themselves will remain perpetually distrustful of each other.
(Lynch, 1712)

Thank you gentlemen
Read full letter at:
https://archive.org/stream/WillieLynchLetter1712/the_willie_lynch_letter_the_making_of_a_slave_1712_djvu.txt

The Black Man in America

There is a major problem with African Americans as a people that have lived through slavery. We have been rape, deceived and confused economically. Our leaders have pointed us in the direction to protesting by marching in the streets. And to complaining, that white people aren't treating us right. African American men have a major problem of uniting economically. Mostly all black men want to be the leader, even if they don't have the knowledge or the temperament to do so. They want to be look up too even if they haven't accomplished a thing.

I believe it comes from slavery, where there was the field slave and the house slave. The field slave had it hard, having to live outside on the plantation in harsh conditions. The house slave lived in the house, where it was warm, and he or she could get plenty to eat. This scenario causes enmity between the house slave and the field slave. The house slave saw himself better than field slave, he dressed better than the field slave. He also didn't socialize very much with the field slave. The house slave also didn't try to help the field slave. He would bring them news about who was going to get sold.

This same pattern is happening today. African American celebrities are the house slaves; they look down on the average Africa American. We are the field slaves and African American celebrities definitely don't socialize with the average African American. African American celebrities socialize with white people. They find it hard to deal with the average African Americans, that are poor because they always have their hands out. Most African Americans celebrities don't give back, but I will give them this, there is no real system for them to give back too. So they can get a return on what they were given, to make sure something is working when they give.

Memorandum to the African Americans

In the 1970's young black men put together gangs instead of corporations. Young black men went into selling the white man drugs in the neighborhood, getting their people hook on drugs. This cause violent that produces black crime on blacks, shooting each other and endangering young African-American children lives, that were playing in the streets, of course, this is still going on. The gangs were making lots of money and spending it foolishly on jewelry, fancy cars, and clothes. Many of them got caught and were given long prison sentences, this is still going on. The prisons are overflowing with black men. Most black men don't know that they were set up to sell drugs and get busted by the white man's D.E.A... Gangs are set up to keep black men from getting and education and becoming a powerful force in mainstream America. The white man wants the black man to become a drug dealer so he can make billions from the war on drugs, both ways meaning; From selling drugs to the drug dealer, and taking away the money, he made from selling the drugs with the law call civil forfeiture.

Civil Forfeiture

Civil forfeiture in the United States, sometimes called civil judicial forfeiture or occasionally civil seizure, is a controversial legal process in which law enforcement officers take assets from persons suspected of involvement with crime or illegal activity without necessarily charging the owners with wrongdoing. (Wikipedia, 2016)

Law enforcement is no more than the overlords. Like the overlords that kept the slaves working and keep watch over them, to make sure they work and keep them from running away. Law enforcement is meant to make sure black men are kept off balance. Watching closely to see if they can get any chance to incarcerate the black man, and take him off the street. Making sure he comes under the judicial system, this is one of the new type of slavery for the black man.

Law enforcement is to make sure black men, don't work together in a disciplined and orderly manner, where they can develop wealth legally. The white man wants the black man to break the laws, so he can keep him as a judicial slave, in the legal system with probation and parole over his head. But most of all white social engineers want the black man uneducated and economically divided. In the secret halls of the white fraternities and frat societies in America, they discuss the legal unity of the black man, it is greatly feared.

Back in the 1900's white men had a deep overpowering fear of a black man marrying his white daughter or a white woman. The movie "Birth of a Nation" the

Memorandum to the African Americans

name was changed from "the Clansman" to make the movie more acceptable. African American men were made to look like clowns in the movie, African Americans were portrayed by white men with black makeup while promoting evil white racism in the nation. The KKK was portrayed as heroes coming to save white people from African Americans that took white people hostage and a black man that want to marry a white woman against her will. Today the movie it's not so threating, the generation that felt this way is dying off. But this thinking made white men come up with ways to keep the black man hope against hope. This has been the key since the Africans laid foot on American soil.

> After the establishment of the Ku Klux Klan in 1867, the number of the lynching of African American increased dramatically. The main objective of the KKK was to maintain white supremacy in the South, which they felt was under threat after their defeat in the Civil War. It has been estimated that between 1880 and 1920, an average of two African Americans a week were lynched in the United States. (Simkin, 2016)

This procedure is to keep the black man from being united and make sure they're fighting among themselves and terrified of the white man, something he has successfully accomplish. The black man must learn the plot set up against him and how to overthrow it.

There is something many black men don't really know, that many illegal immigrants were let into this country, to undermine the African Americans who would not work for low wages. The deep problem is that the black man didn't have a system in place to take advantage of this opportunity, and white social engineers knew this. Immigrants came to the country and took advantage of the black man lack of economic unity and a system to control the dollars in his community. Immigrants have come and obtained loans that the black man couldn't get and still can't get. They built a business in our community and took that money to white communities, where they have set up residence.

Right now if I go to the black man with an economic plan, the field slave, and the house slave, slave mentality will come up. I believe these walls can be broken down between us. But there must be leadership, discipline, and sacrifice. There must be millions of black men that will need to see beyond their nose; meaning stop worrying only about themselves and join together economically.

See the larger picture for the future of young African Americans, that need a constructive path to follow. With positive thinking and a wholesome plan, that

Memorandum to the African Americans

takes into account economic forces that drive the markets we participate in, and that plan is capitalism. By working with a capitalist plan and most of all understanding capitalism, we can use it to our advantage. We must own and share in the profits of this plan, in an economical revolution to bring wealth to the African American families, with capitalism.

The African American Family

In the days of slavery, African Americans were the property of the white man and could be sold at the white man whim. As slaves, African Americans had no say in the matter. The black man as a Father was castrated as a man, the white man could take his family and sell them and sell the black man himself as stud just like a horse. ***Willie Lynch wrote to white slave owners:***

> Breed the mare and the stud until you have the desired offspring. Then you can turn the stud to freedom until you need him again. Train the female horse whereby she will eat out of your hand, and she will, in turn, train the infant horse to eat out of your hand also. When it comes to breaking the uncivilized nigger, use the same process, but vary the degree and step up the pressure, so as to do a complete reversal of the mind. Take the meanest and most restless nigger, strip him of his clothes in front of the remaining male niggers, the female, and the nigger infant, tar and feather him, tie each leg to a different horse faced in opposite directions, set him afire and beat both horses to pull him apart in front of the remaining nigger. The next step is to take a bullwhip and beat the remaining nigger male to the point of death, in front of the female and the infant. Don't kill him, but put the fear of God in him, for he can be useful for future breeding. (Lynch 1712)

This evil that was perpetrated on the Blackman, would detract him from his family, the burden of losing his family was heartbreaking and painful. Always in the back of his mind, he had to realize that his family was the property of the white man. Today many black men are detracted from their families there either in prison, separated or divorced. I believe this is something that was carried over from slavery. This isn't to give the black man and excuse; but a reason for him to bear in mind, of what he can easily be reduced to an indolent, not taking care of his family. Many don't have a good education, alcohol, drugs, and crime have defined them. They are pushed by their peers when they are young, pressured to be with the ghetto status quo, a gang member or a drug dealer.

Memorandum to the African Americans

This pressure is in the DNA of slavery that haunts the black man; he has no true economic foundation among other black men. Our thinking is how can I get a job with the white man. Leaving the majority of black men out of the prosperity picture. Our idea of making it is to do a crime and not get caught, or getting a job or having a successful business to take care of my family. Most black men want to argue about anything, this is a defensive mechanism to cover up their inability to understand something, or just to get out of a situation they are uncomfortable with. There isn't one ounce of unity for African American men unless it is as a gang member. This path leads to drugs, crime, mischief, death and false comradery. This is a legacy that is the cycle of poverty, for African American children to grow up with. In the neighborhood of these gang's members, this is the only thing they are persuaded to join.

The gang leaders leading young African Americans their friends, brothers, sisters to prison and death, living by the code of the streets, and running with guns in their possession. Never realizing they are no more than agents of destruction, for the white man. Gang members are breaking down the family unit among African Americans. The white man produced this behavior through subconscious social engineering, hoping that these young African American men will never wake up to the truth, and if they ever do wake up, shoot them on sight.

At this time of the writing of this book, the white man has nothing to worry about. Young African American men will kill each other without a second thought. The African American family is a dysfunctional family because of many extenuating circumstances. The foundation of the African American family is built on shaky ground; we have not developed a culture among ourselves, that will support wealth. We take the crumbs that fall from the white man's table. We take the money we get and give it right back to the white man. We are therefore no more than consumers' slaves. Mothers and Fathers teaching the children the same pattern through examples. Telling their children to get a good education and after you do that then try to get a good job. There is nothing about generating wealth and the ownership of capital, with the unity of African American businesses.

African-American children leave the house and head out into the streets. This is what has developed street life in the community, there is no direction in the community. The streets are dangerous because African-American parents don't care what their children are doing. They want the children to leave them alone. They have been working to pay the rent, put food on the table and clothes on their

Memorandum to the African Americans

children backs. African American parents feel they have a right for their children to leave them alone because of this. The time of African American children are spent in aimless pursuits, and when they grow up; they have nothing to show for it.

Many young African American girls get pregnant at a young age without the maturity or capital(money) to raise a child. The child suffers from this lack of maturity and capital (money). The father is nowhere to be found, that is why there is so much mental illness in the African-American community. The mother is frustrated because she still wants to do things she did before she had a baby. Not understanding the repercussions from having a baby, the cost in time, the need for growing up herself, and developing maturity. She also doesn't understand that a baby will not make a man love her, or keep that man in her life because of the baby. Young African American girls develop quickly and they effortlessly fall in so-called love.

Easily seduce into intercourse and believing lies told by the male she is with. Believing in fairy tale lies, that they're going to be together forever until she tells him that she is pregnant. Usually, the male is as young as she is, with no job to support her or the child. This is the anatomy of the African American family evolving in American neighborhoods, producing the ghetto plantations.

Black men in America must unite on an economic basis, that includes integrity, discipline, honor, respect and love for one another. This must be the core values of our relationship in raising African American children in our families. Teaching them how to work together, by the examples we display through our interaction with one another. Black men must take responsibility for our actions. But most of all we need to come together, with a plan of redemption changing how we live our lives and raise our families.

Black men need to love and respect the mother of our children. The black woman must have leadership from the black man, that doesn't threaten her love toward her man. The black man should never perpetrate violent on the black woman. He must show her why; she must carry herself as a lady in public life. And show her how much he appreciates her love and caring ways. He must be a teacher of his family showing understanding, teaching his children the importance of education. And why it is important to unite economically with other African Americans in business and social life.

The development of culture is needed in African America family experience. If the black man is going to enjoy the wealth of this nation on a mass scale. He

Memorandum to the African Americans

must implement the very things I am pointing out. If the African-Americans unite, fear will run through every corner of the white man's world. This type of revolution would shake America and the world to its core. The black man would receive respect and economic power. African Americans stepping up to the plate with this type of a plan, would hit home runs. White women would be throwing themselves at the black man, of course, stupid black men would fall for this, and potentially destroy the plan, that we would be working toward. Understand I have no hatred or dislike for white people, I love them and all people of the world. But this is about the African-American Family and raising African Americans out of poverty. We need to be careful about white people, in our relationship making sure they are genuine and not just curious, and working to manipulate us and trying to undermine our capitalistic plan.

The African American Woman

The Black woman has carried the African American family throughout our history. She has been a rock, enduring the hardship of hope and the anxiety of pray. Being concern with where will the next meal come from? Where is that man that she relying on to feed the family; and give her some attention. The black woman has cried, quietly in the night, for God to give her strength, to make it through another day. She is not ashamed to turn to the white man for help, of course, this has always been the plan of the white man.

Willie Lynch wrote to white slave owners:

> We have reversed the relationship in her natural uncivilized state she would have a strong dependency on the uncivilized nigger male, and she would have a limited protective tendency toward her independent male offspring and would raise male off springs to be dependent like her. Nature had provided for this type of balance. We reversed nature by burning and pulling a civilized nigger apart and bull whipping the other to the point of death, all in her presence. By her being left alone, unprotected, with the male image destroyed, the ordeal caused her to move from her psychological dependent state to a frozen independent state. In this frozen psychological state of independence, she will raise her male and female offspring in reversed roles. For fear of the young male's life she will psychologically train him to be mentally weak and dependent, but physically strong. Because she has become psychologically independent, she will train her female off springs to be psychological independent. What have you got? You've got the

Memorandum to the African Americans

nigger women out front and the nigger man behind and scared. This is a perfect situation of sound sleep and economic. Before the breaking process, we had to be alertly on guard at all times. (Lynch 1712)

From the days of slavery, the black woman was made to be a leader of the family; instead of the black man, in order for the white man to control the black family. The black man has no support system, he's too busy fighting his own brothers in the streets, trying to show his manhood, with his braggadocios nature and fake hopes. Working to get high on, alcohol, drugs, weed or something. Having no economic plan, this leads to inferior thinking. And the economic plan doesn't even enter his mind, the white man's world has beat so many black men down that their numb. Without unity among us and education, we are bewildered, leaving the black woman to fend for herself and her children.

In **1967 more than a half (56%) of Black families headed by single women** lived below the national poverty level compared to **33% of all families** in America headed by single women. During the decade of the 1990s the poverty rate of families headed by Black single mothers **dropped from 48%** in 1990 to its lowest point **(34%) in 2000**. The economic downturn in the decade from 2000 to 2010 increased the Black family poverty rate to **39% by 2010**. Since 2010 the Black family poverty rate **decreased slightly to 37% by 2014**. Although the actual disparity between Black single mother families and all single mother families has always been lower than that between all family types the adjustments (increases and decreases) in disparity over the decades have been fairly similar. (BLACK DEMOGRAPHIC NEWS, 2014)

The Black woman suffers wishing and dreaming of wealth and luxury, that her man cannot provide for her and the children. However, she carries on doing the best she can do for her family. Wishing for a rich man or just a good man, that would love her and provide for her children. The great sadness in all this is, many black women have been left to raise a young African America boy to be a man, by a black woman standards. Many African American men love their mother dearly, she has been there for them through the up and downs. While the young man is trying to make it in the white man's world. So many have fallen into the same trap of crime as their father before him. A trap laid by the white man to keep African

Memorandum to the African Americans

American men in a mental illusion and mental illness, so that we can't work together.

The Black woman has done a great job as far as being a mother. But when she has to be a father too, it begins to complicate the life of the African American boy. He wants to know what is the real role of an African American man in the family. African American boy wonders why his father is so elusive in his life. The father may come by and argue with his mother and now he's gone. The young African America boy gets the wrong message, and thinks is this how a relationship is supposed to be with a woman? There are stable African American families but they are few. The African American parents are set at odds because of the culture that has to develop within African American experience through the slave mentality. The African American woman needs the proper help to raise an African American boy, she needs to stop trying to be his father. But she can't help it, the black man is too busy running the streets, pretending he doing something with his life.

With that being said, the African American man must learn how to be a faithful parent, and understand how important it is to build and economic infrastructure in the African American family nationwide. This can only be done by powerful leadership and the development of an economic plan of unity within the African-American experience. This would allow the African American woman to focus on raising her daughter to be a mother.

Also, she can nurture all her children, and be a great wife and a helpmate to her husband. Within this economic revolution, the black woman would be prompt, to put together events that would gender family ties. Gathering with other black women to set family standards of the culture revolution, that would be set in etiquette within our economic capitalistic system. I thank God for the strength of the Black woman because it is truly amazing and without it, the African Americans wouldn't have come as far as we have.

The African American Children

African American children are blessed to be in America, but the question becomes apparent. Why, are they so uneducated and poverty surround our very existence? Of course, there are factors in our neighborhoods one of them is our public schools are run down (crumbs from the white man's table), the curriculum is inferior, it will not take African American children to the next level. It is a system set up by the white man to keep African-American children from entering the mainstream America in large numbers.

Memorandum to the African Americans

African American parents are too busy trying to make a living to even give a dam. They feel since they brought the child into the world. The child now has to make it on their own in the white man's world, and few and far between can do that. It's really the parent's responsibility for guiding, encouraging and inspire their children to pursue constructive pursuits of their choosing. This also means whatever they think they want to be; the parents should help them in their youth to find out what it takes. To obtain the basic means to get them started, and point out the talent they see within them.

Young African American children watch too much television and eat too much junk food. Their becoming overweight, falling into gangs, where the leadership of the gangs, leads straight to prison and death. They want to fit in by wearing clothes like gang members, with their pants hanging down and their attitude the same way. Their pants hanging down with no etiquette whatsoever, and peer pressure to be tough and someone in the gangs always have a gun, that leads to trouble. Only an "African American Parent Association" can put a stop to gangs from organizing in the community and nationwide, only parents can stop this. African American parents must confront African American children and especially the young men, they live in the house with their parents, and hide their association with the gang, also hiding the weapons they possess.

There is a larger picture here that can only be addressed by African Americans. This trend started with drugs being pushed into the Black community by the white man. Knowing young black men want to get their hands on money and plenty of it. The white man seduced young black men into selling drugs, they allow them to buy wholesale drugs and sell them to the community. The white man has also sold them illegal guns to kill other African Americans. The situation is something that young African Americans are unaware of that their being set up. Set up to sell the drugs, then the D.E.A runs in and bust the gang and confiscate all the money, guns, and items they purchase. This is the true agenda behind the "War on Drugs" this is a hidden agenda, that comes down to civil seizure.

> We believe that the mass criminalization of people of color, particularly young African American men, is as profound a system of racial control as the Jim Crow laws were in this country until the mid-1960s. (Drug Policy Alliance, 2016)

This way the young African American male, didn't know he was working for the white man and destroying his own family in the process. What a diabolical

Memorandum to the African Americans

concept, yet brilliant, an urban genocide without the victims knowing or understanding what's going on. Young African American men just walking willingly into the trap, thinking that they're the ones that came up with the idea of selling drugs and carrying guns. While surveillance takes place until the suckers have amassed enough cash and kill enough rivals. Then law enforcement runs in and takes all the cash and items they purchased with the ill-gotten gain. Taking all of them to prison, providing a relief in the community, because of the violent and death this genocide conjured.

> One in six black men had been incarcerated as of 2001. If current trends continue, one in three black males born today can expect to spend time in prison during his lifetime. (NAACP, 2015)

The white man is the producer and black man was the salesman (the dealer of drugs). But now many immigrants have taken over the drug trade. While prisons overflow with African American men caught up in the drug trap, like a rat caught in a trap, trying to get a piece of cheese. Knowledge and leadership can hopefully bring the Black man out of the trap.

African American children don't realize that they are set up to fail in the white man's system. Racism is the key to inferior teaching in public schools. The public school system is no more than a babysitting institution. This has always kept the door of opportunity closed for the majority of African Americans. Without adult African Americans understanding, that we as a people must fight racism from an economic standpoint, and not by always protesting.

The majority of African Americans will continue in poverty; protesting is no more than begging the white man to do what is right. He will always keep us in the cotton fields of poverty as consumers' slaves and on the ghetto plantations, receiving only crumbs that fall from the white man's table. Or to say it in a political way, waiting for the trickle-down theory, where the trickle has never reached the African American community.

Many African American children are raised around drug dealing, drug addiction, drug addicts, gang members and prostitution. On top of this, an African American child must deal with racism and immigrants invading our community, schools, and jobs. The deck is stack against the African American child; a wake-up call is needed for the African American families. However, change can't happen for the African American families without the participation of the majority of African Americans joining in the economic revolution.

Memorandum to the African Americans

We have secure civil rights and voting rights for African Americans, who stood up to the white racist's system, with the leadership of many black leaders. But especially Martin Luther King Jr. marching through the streets of America. The problem is there was no economic plan for businesses among African Americans, and a plan for an inheritance for the next generation. Martin Luther King Jr. was going to have a March on Washington for jobs. There will never be a way out of poverty if we look to the white man to give us a job in his businesses. He may do it for a few of us, so he can say, "look at my token." But it won't be for the majority, and why should he, when we need to do things for ourselves.

African American children grow up thinking; I need a job, instead of thinking I need to go into business with my African American brother or sister, this is the pathway to wealth. Of course, there is no foundation lay down for them to do so. Our parents and our leaders have only one- dimensional thinking; get a job and or protest. African American children need a new pathway in America, learning to work together. We need to take the new coming generation and lead them to waters of prosperity. By teaching them to bathed in unity, discipline, respect, honor, integrity, love and leadership within the African American people.

This is easier said than done, but it isn't impossible. When African American children are trained properly great things will come about. There is a great deal of creativity in young African Americans, only when it is nurture will it come into full fruition. Blues, Jazz, Rock & Roll, and Hip Hop all came from the creativity of young African Americans, and many inventions from our ancestors. But the white man enjoys all the fruits of our creativity and have given us crumbs to live on from our creativity. I'm sure if young African Americans are led on a business path, they can bring African American people out of poverty, receiving the lion's share of our creativity.

There are many African American leaders that have tried to deal with the plight of the African Americans. But not one of them could bring the African Americans out of poverty. Most African Americans and African Americans leaders don't really understand the white man, as much as they think they do. The white man is watching our every move. Watching all the moves African Americans make and taking action to keep them in mental slavery. They have secret meetings to talk about African Americans and anyone that looks like a leader, they make a plan of action to see what is needed to make the leader ineffective.

Memorandum to the African Americans

The white man understands the important of leadership, this is what has gotten him to a dominant place in the world. White people banding together to follow the orders of a leader. If you don't have a head you can't think, white people understand this principle. Whereas African Americans, when they were freed from slavery develop and attitude. That they didn't want anyone telling them what to do. The white man has told us what to do all our life through slavery. We or not about to listen to a black man or woman, tell us what to do even if it was good for us. This is the same attitude today, that has been carried over since slavery, and attitude that definitely needs to change.

African American Leaders

Let's look at a few African American leaders:

Harriet Tubman Writer, abolitionist 1820-1913 As an abolitionist, she acted as an intelligence gatherer, refugee organizer, raid leader, nurse, revival speaker, and fundraiser.

Booker T. Washington Political leader, educator, author 1856-1915 One of the dominant figures in African-American history from 1890 to 1915; did much to improve the friendship and working relationship between the races. And founded the National Negro Business League in 1901

George Washington Carver Plant scientist 1860-1943 Taught former slaves farming techniques for self-sufficiency; known for suggesting hundreds of uses for the peanut, and other plants.

Marcus Garvey Publisher, journalist, entrepreneur 1887-1940 Best remembered as a champion of the "Back-to-Africa" movement. He was Jamaican and deported for mail fraud.

Elijah Muhammad Leader of the Nation of Islam with 100's of thousands of followers, he claimed to be the Messenger of Allah.

Malcolm X Civil rights leader 1925-1965 A.K.A. El-Hajj Malik El-Shabazz; one-time Minister of Nation of Islam. One of the founders of Organization of Afro-American Unity.

Martin Luther King Jr. Civil rights activist, minister, Nobel laureate 1929-1968 Won the Nobel Peace Prize, PH.D. in Theology, Presidential Medal of Freedom

Memorandum to the African Americans

before the assassination in 1968; known for advocating non-violence, racial equality; a peacemaker, martyr.

This is to show just a few African American leaders there are many more. In the 1960's the Black Power Movement began, African Americans stood up for their civil rights. There were many black leaders that starting surfacing with their organization and leadership. Many ideas have been put forth in many African American organizations over hundreds of years. Yet there is still a great deal of poverty in the lives of most African Americans.

Most of the African American leaders ignore the white man's cunningness, surveillance, and calculations on keeping African Americans down. Look at a time in history, at what white people did to successful African Americans in 1921. In the black community of Tulsa, Oklahoma, the Greenwood District, it was also called Black Wall Street. This riot was started when a white teenage girl accused a black teenage boy of touching her behind. I believe the dirty KKK set this up, with the help of that white teenage girl. Plus, the Black community didn't touch the white teenage girl's, behind. The federal government didn't send the National Guards in until the district was burned down. The federal government never repaid African Americans for this white racist riot hurricane, that destroyed Greenwood District.

Tulsa race riot

The Tulsa race riot was a large-scale, racially motivated pogrom on May 31 and June 1, 1921, in which a group of whites attacked the black community of Tulsa, Oklahoma. The Greenwood District, the wealthiest black community in the United States, was burned to the ground. Over the course of 16 hours, more than 800 people were admitted to local white hospitals with injuries, the two black hospitals were burned down, and police arrested and detained more than 6,000 black Greenwood residents at three local facilities. An estimated 10,000 blacks were left homeless, and 35 city blocks composed of 1,256 residences were destroyed by fire, resulting in over $26 million in damages. The official count of the dead by the Oklahoma Department of Vital Statistics was 39, but other estimates of black fatalities vary from 55 to about 300.

Memorandum to the African Americans

The events of the massacre were long omitted from local and state histories: "The Tulsa race riot of 1921 was rarely mentioned in history books, classrooms or even in private. Blacks and whites alike grew into middle age unaware of what had taken place." With the number of survivors declining, in 1996, the state legislature commissioned a report to establish the historical record of the events, and acknowledge the victims and damages to the black community. Released in 2001, the report included the commission's recommendations for some compensatory actions, most of which were not implemented by the state and city governments. The state passed legislation to establish some scholarships for descendants of survivors, economic development of Greenwood, and a memorial park to the victims in Tulsa. The latter was dedicated in 2010. (Wikipedia, 2016)

This is what white people did to successful African Americans in 1921. This is something we must be aware of today. African American leaders have to deal with uneducated African Americans by the millions. Who have no sense of direction because poverty has kept them desperate and hungry. The leaders today are silence, with a Black President Obama having been in the White House, which African Americans are proud of and we're greatly excited. But we are still in poverty; can the black men in American be brought out of poverty? Can you stop a pig from waddling in the mire?

As long as there is no economic unity with African Americans nationwide. And uneducated African Americans living in the mire of poverty, and refusing to clean themselves up and their children with higher education, and with an economic revolution of capitalism. The subconscious chains of slavery that have bound us, will continue to bind us to poverty. African American leaders can only get a few African Americans to follow them.

This is because many African Americans look at white people and long to be just like them. And when African-Americans become wealthy they hang out with white people. They find it hard to give back because it will only go into the vortex of poverty. There is no real system for their giving to produce positive results. Out of all the leaders, I believe Brooker T. Washington founder of the National Negro Business League would be the close thing I think that could help African Americans. But his organization left out and inheritance component.

But just like all other organizations that became of non-effect, too many always relied on the involvement of the white man directly or indirectly. I'm not

Memorandum to the African Americans

saying to do it without the white man, this is his country and his system. But you must be as cunning as he is in using his system to obtain wealth. Just as we receive civil rights by using his own words against him. Such words as "We hold these truths to be self-evident, that all men are created equal, that they are endowed by their Creator with certain unalienable Rights, that among these are Life, Liberty and the pursuit of Happiness." African American leaders came to realize white people live by these writings and that such documents are contracts. However, the masses of African Americans don't realize it; paper money is no more than a contractual agreement. Which is the white man's system for the purpose of transacting business more readily, which paper money and plastic cards execute?

This becomes a crucial problem in the African American psyche believing money will change their lives. Understand what I'm trying to point out, money is only a means to an end. The system to obtain the money is what is important not the money itself. African Americans think that if I could just get my hands on some money, it will change my circumstances, and it would temporarily. But soon it would be gone, you need to have continual money coming in to sustain the change in your life. And if the money is obtained illegally, it just a matter of time before you get caught and jailed. This is a type of thinking a leader of African Americans has to deal with when organizing African Americans.

African American leaders that made a different

Harriet Tubman, went back to the South 19 times to take African Americans to freedom. Many were afraid, they went on anyway, but if any wanted to turn back she had a rule; go to freedom or you'll die to try to turn back, and she never lost a passenger.

Brooker T. Washington, founded the National Negro Business League, this was very promising; it established several black businesses nationwide. The market forces change the landscape with the depression of the 1930's.

George Washington Carver, a great scientist understood the power of the peanut. Producing several products and taught African Americans the powers of them. But there was no system to incorporate it, for the coming generations to take advantage and become wealthy, the white man cunningly made sure that it wouldn't happen.

Elijah Muhammad, Leader of the Nation of Islam took men out of prison, like Malcom Little who became Malcom X and change them with discipline and purpose through his version of Islam, he also open businesses nationwide. The

Memorandum to the African Americans

Nation of Islam was disbanded by his son Wallace D. Muhammad. Until Louis Farrakhan came to is senses and restore the Nation of Islam.

Malcolm X, once a national spokesman for the Nation of Islam. Change his name to El-Hajj Malik El-Shabazz and help form the Organization of Afro-American Unity. El-Shabazz came to understand the importance of African American unity. But before he could truly expound and implement it, he was assassinated by men from the Nation of Islam, with the help of the FBI.

Martin Luther King Jr., was a prolific leader, he attended Boston University and received a Ph.D. degree in theology on June 5, 1955. He was a Nobel laureate, he put together a successful boycott so African Americans wouldn't have to ride in the back of the bus. Though he became a martyr, there was no economic plan left for African Americans. Just more protesting which will always keep us poor. He put together the "Poor People Campaign" in 1968 for jobs and economic justice, he was assassinated two weeks before it was set to happen.

These few African American leaders I have selected to show that the pathway for African Americans has been a hard road to freedom without prosperity. Only a few African Americans have obtained prosperity, compare to how many African Americans live in America. This is the history of African Americans since we have lived in America. However, I will not lay all the blame at the feet of the white man. African Americans on a national level must put together a national plan, that includes all or at lease most African Americans in order to enjoy the wealth of this land, again there must be a system in place. I address this in the "Solution" as I write "Memorandum to the African Americans."

Leadership in the African American community must be placed on many levels. The place it must start is in the African American home. The children of African Americans will need special education in math, science, technology and engineering, these courses must be learned outside of public school. The African American Organization wants to address this problem with the "African American Training Center." In the center, African-American children must understand how to follow leadership and how important it is to have leadership. Mothers and Fathers have to reinforce the significant of education, also the coming generation will be the ones running the capitalistic system, to bring about the change. These values must be instilled at a young age so that the principles, can take root to produce the desired state of affairs. African American children need to be reminded about the effects of racism and how to combat it.

Memorandum to the African Americans

Institutionalize Racism

Institutionalize Racism is a highly formalized system that the white man has put in place to discriminate against African Americans. There are code words, things to look out for when African Americans are applying for jobs and looking to use services, or when and African Americans walks into a store. Your name also identifies you and sends up red flags. This type of racism is under the radar and when most, white people are confronted with it, they play dumb, as if they didn't realize it. White racism has basically made the Presidency of Barak Obama of non-effect, because of the white racism of Republican Party, he can't get anything through Congress.

However, he handed the Congress over to Republicans, so they could implement this type of racism. Obama ignored the will and need of the people, for a legacy, he hoped to establish through his implementation of the Affordable Care Act. White people that voted him into office began to turn from the Democrats, Obama should have first used his honeymoon period in the Presidency, to get jobs for the people and help small businesses instead of giving unemployment to the majority of the population. Republicans began a campaign of institutionalizing racism of which they succeed in. They campaign to deny people of color voting rights through crafty political tactics. Institutionalized racism is in all aspects of America and even in the prison system. The key to institutionalize racism is to keep the Black man, uneducated and fighting among themselves and interested in doing a crime.

This way the Black man is kept in the chains of an illusion of being free and covered with the fog of desperation. The white man has accomplished this, along with the Black man hating his own black brother, beating his beautiful black woman. As well as speaking to her in very demeaning tones, and not taking care of the children he fathered and having to pay child support to the government. This is to the satisfaction of the white man that engineered institutionalize racism.

Most black men don't understand how important the black woman is to define, our culture and our family values. The white man knows that the black man is deaf, dumb, and blind to economic unity. Therefore, he takes the purchasing power of the black man to make him into a consumer slave. And uses the police department to harass him in his own community, to keep the fog of desperation in his pathway.

Memorandum to the African Americans

The white man is also teaching immigrants that come to this country to use institutionalize racism against African Americans. Speaking to them in the back room with codes and examples. Tell them that Blacks are thieves and robbers and cannot be trusted, also other African Americans believe the same, because of this African Americans have the highest unemployment rate. With this stereotype, many of us have to suffer from the metaphor. This new tool, institutionalize racism is working very well for the white man.

Many African-American men have been killed right in public by the police, it's no more than white police lynching. They are acquitted of all charges only because he was a black man. Institutionalized racism has allowed the police officers to go free. Organizations start protesting on the street about these killings, the protesting and marching sometimes make a change, only when politicians see that they may lose the election. Institutionalize racism is the new key for denying opportunities to African Americans and getting white police officers acquitted, also uniting white racist people.

The major problem is the black man has no strategy to deal with this type of racism, too many are caught in the moment; meaning trying to stay out of jail and being unjustly shot. When they are stopped by the white racist police officer, who looking for approval from his fellow officers, that he or she has arrest a black person. But great approval comes when he has killed a black man. This isn't said openly, but this is acknowledged in the back room and is a higher power of institutionalized racism. ***Take a look at this institutionalize racism:***

(1) If a black person and a white person each commit a crime; the black person is more likely to be arrested. This is due in part to the fact that black people are more heavily policed. (The discrepancy could also be driven by overt racism, more frequent illegal searches of black people, or an increased willingness to let non-blacks off with a warning.)

(2) When black people are arrested for a crime, they are convicted more often than white people arrested for the same crime. (This discrepancy could also be due to racial bias on the part of judges and jurors.)

Racial disparities in the application of criminal justice are not the only source of differential incarceration rates. Poverty, geography, and lacking educational and career opportunities all likely play a role. These factors exacerbate the effects of systemic racism and feeds the cycle of

Memorandum to the African Americans

incarceration, joblessness, and poverty that plagues some segments of the black population. (Farbota, 2015)

Most white people know and understand this institutionalize racism. They talk about it when no African Americans are around. And let each other know, what is expected, when it comes to dealing with African Americans, they are told outright racism can't be shown. Because it can have devastating consequences for those who engage in it. Not all white people accept institutionalize racism, and there are quite a few fair mind white Americans, that stand up for freedom, justice and equality for all Americans. For today's white people, it's not like it was back when their ancestors could use outright racism. It must now be Institutionalize racism, because of the changing times and the attitude of the Federal government and global exposure. To African Americans, I say to you; "beware and come to together to overcome institutionalize racism."

Social Engineering

I want to briefly touch, upon social engineering upon African Americans. As I have spoken of all the immigrants that have come into this country especially from Mexico. It was socially engineered by the Republican party; they wanted cheaper labor. African-Americans wanted more pay and a higher salary for minimal jobs they were doing. The white business owners also wanted cheaper labor in construction jobs. Under George Bush Jr., the Mexicans were allowed to cross the border in the millions. That allow the white business community to hire the Mexicans for cheaper wages.

The Mexicans were glad to work for these cheaper wages, because in Mexico, the wages were 50 times less than what they're getting in America. They also could send money back home, save money and go back home and buy property in their country. Now today millions upon millions of illegal Mexicans have come to this country. They want higher wages and the Republicans now want them deported back to Mexico. The white business owner is doing business with China, India and Mexico and any foreign country where they can get cheaper laborers, to produce their products or services, sending Americans jobs out of the country. Mexicans have also enrolled in public schools, you can barely find and African American child in the public school.

Memorandum to the African Americans

Mexicans have taken jobs and gotten into a position of power where they don't hire African Americans. Mexicans have now tapped into institutionalized racism and discrimination against African Americans. African Americans have accepted them with open arms. The problem is they're becoming like the white man. And their children want to fight with African American children in the public schools. I do not hate Mexicans or any people, I love them and the food of their culture. But these are facts, African Americans must beware of this, and address this with economic unity among African Americans.

Memorandum to the African Americans

Attitude

Attitude; is defined as a settled way of thinking or feeling about someone or something, typically one that is reflected in a person's behavior.

I want to take a scripture from the Bible to express an attitude to bring out an understanding for African Americans. In Isaiah 55:9 it is written, "for as the heavens are higher than the earth, so are my ways higher than your ways, and my thoughts than your thoughts." Attitude is a way of thinking that is reflected by behavior. In this scripture, God is showing man his thoughts and his behavior is far above man.

The way you think will show your behavior and thought process. God's is far superior to man as far as the heavens are above us. I speak to the African American, to look at how we think and the way we, behave. It's not because of the white man we live in poverty, it is the way we think and behave. Our thought tends to survival and not to living. Our thinking is "I got to make it on my own", we don't think about working together, with other African Americans. So that there can be wealth and an inheritance for the future generations that will come after us.

Poverty is for small minded thinking people that cannot come to light of developing wealth. In order to see the larger picture, Malcom X travel to Africa, it expanded his thinking. He came up with the "Organization of Afro-American Unity" he realized how important it was for African Americans to come together on all levels of existence. Before he came to this revelation he thought and act like the black man in the streets of Boston Massachusetts.

Malcom X says in his autobiography:

> This was my first really big step toward self-degradation: when I endured all of that pain, literally burning my flesh to have it look like a white man's hair. I had joined that multitude of Negro men and women in America who are brainwashed into believing that the black people are "inferior"-and white people "superior"-that they will even violate and mutilate their God-created bodies to try to look "pretty" by white standards. (Haley, 2016)

Malcom X came to understand how powerful thoughts and behavior shape our destiny. The attitude in the African American community leads to the very thing

Memorandum to the African Americans

that Malcom X came to experience, before his rise in the Nation of Islam and the world stage. The question becomes; how can we change the attitude of African Americans? So that African Americans can reflect a more positive attitude. A positive attitude that will chart a pathway out of poverty? The important of this cannot be express vividly enough, our nationwide attitude is what has kept us trap in poverty, and on the ghetto plantations and in the projects prison, picking consumer cotton.

Take a look at the thinking of young African Americans. Our bright ones have gone rogue because the dumb ones that have use scare tactics to get them into gangs. Giving them examples where they wear their pants hanging down. Teaching young African Americans to act tough and dangerous so that nobody better mess with them or they will hurt or kill that person. They don't know that this is a trick of the white man. So he can identify the dumb ones and most all of the stupid ones that are carrying guns. The hope of the white man is, that the gang member will kill his own brother and sell drugs to his community until he is caught. After this takes place he can put them in prison, and take all their money and confiscate their goods. This attitude travels through the African American experience.

As Malcom X point this out in his time, which still exist until this day. African Americans are trying to live by the white man standards. The problem which is even more unsettling is that African Americans today don't know that they are brain-wash. Enjoying the deceit, without knowing their attitude has brought them to their captor. The captor has blinded them, keeping them dumb, brainwashed and numb within his ghetto plantations. When our ancestors were brought to this country it was illegal to teach an African to read or write. The white man has always understood that knowledge is power. If you can keep a human being from knowledge, you can control that person, by telling them whatever you desire, and they will be persuaded to believe you.

The attitude of African Americans has kept them tied to falsehood, you can't get most, black men to read a book. We believe whatever the white man tells us. It like as if we as a people are under a hypnotic enchantment. Unable to break the spell because secret fear has held us captive. In an invisible cage stifling our thoughts as a people with the stench of slavery and the lack of awareness. It's vital to know our strength and weaknesses so that we can stop being exploited, by our own negative attitude toward one another. Unless we develop higher thoughts and behavior to accompany the higher thoughts. Poverty will forever dangle around or

Memorandum to the African Americans

necks, we need to stop acting uppity, like were somebody in America. Yes, we must be level headed and caring for one another. But this doesn't happen without leadership and a firm economic plan, that addresses higher thoughts, and behavior, that can be enacted through the African American community.

We could also use the help of African American celebrities, with the development of our attitude; I say this with a grain of salt. African American celebrities are right up there with white people, feeding into institutionalized racism against African Americans. I will give them this escape clause, that there is no real system for them to make a valuable contribution to verifiable results in any African American economic plan.

African Americans attitude can bring about trends through our creativity, sending a social revolution into the African American community. A revolution that will touch the lives of our mother, father, sister, brother, friends and relatives. The revolution of economic unity can bring prosperity to their lives. In a new social order by developing the capitalistic process in their social lives.

We need to show that there is an attitude adjustment happening in our events and community. And that this social order has changed the way African-American addresses and treat each other. With a changed atmosphere filled with laughter, joy and most of all purpose. When reading this many will say, "you are living in a dream world." But I would submit to anyone reading this.

I would express to you with the attitude that Martin Luther King said, "I have a dream." Where people believe, it's possible for a dream to come true. And at one time ask the question can a black man be President of the United States of America? So I don't think it so far- fetched to think on this high level. And for African Americans to change their attitude and become economically savvy, so I can say "I have a revelation".

I Have a Revelation

My mission in this revelation is to get the average African American to become a member of the African American Organization. I want them to be a stockholder and to know that in this organization we are capitalists. As I began this subject, "Attitude" with my ways are higher than your ways and my thoughts higher than your thoughts. Plus, the meaning of attitude which is a settled way of thinking or feeling about someone or something, typically one that is reflected in a person's behavior. I believe, I was called to be a leader of African Americans. But I

Memorandum to the African Americans

am under no illusion of how challenging this calling is, many are called, but few are chosen. There is one thing I know, that this calling continues to beat upon my soul. And the voice of God, by the power of the Spirit, confirms it every time I try to turn into another direction, I'm directed back to lead African Americans. So I must heed the calling, even if I'm laughed at, and ridiculed before I go to my grave.

As I write this "Memorandum to the African Americans" let me note. I have had experience leading African Americans in 1992 to get jobs and contracts in a burndown community of Los Angeles, South Central. In 1993 I advocated that African Americans must invest in themselves. The grave will close my hope, but I will never change my purpose for African Americans. I have a revelation; African Americans must invest in themselves, in order to leave the ghetto plantations. Meaning take the money, that you have in your possession, no matter how much, accumulate, control capital, invest in yourself while developing wealth. Unite under one organization, and provide a dividend to all members of the organization.

This is a revelation that has been revealed to me, and it like standing at the foot of mount Everest and looking up. The attitude in the African American community is I have no money to invest. African Americans will continue to say, "I need the money for my necessities," this is where the hard climb comes in. This is about the attitude of the average African American, the challenge to lead them to wealth building and prosperity. The attitude that we have is why we are still living in a ghetto state of mind, not understanding it takes leadership and sacrifice on the behalf of African Americans.

The first level to climb this mountain is African American will say, "I have no money," the average African American must learn to think out of the box. Taking what you do have and making the most of it by uniting nationwide. In this climb, the first order of business is to accumulate capital, (save money) and develop wealth through capitalism. I think this is very challenging for the average African American, to wrap his or her mind around this plan. And when the white man gets wind of it, his fear will transfer into terror. For him, the unity of African Americans economically must never happen. Remember what happen in Tulsa, Oklahoma, the Greenwood District, white people couldn't stand the prosperity of African Americans.

The white man will go into underground meetings, using the FBI and the CIA to infiltrate the organization, to see if we have broken any laws. The next step they

Memorandum to the African Americans

will take, can we stop them with the racketeering laws, or with the Securities and Exchange Commission (SEC), also the Commodity Futures Trading Commission, and see if there are any tax evasion laws broken. For them, the bottom line is that the average African American must be kept on the ghetto plantations and picking consumer cotton. It is highly profitable for the white man to keep Africa Americans in the ghettos, so he thinks; with a heavy police present.

The second level of the mountain to climb, is the selling of drugs, drug use, gangs, firearms, prostitution, lack of education, and alcohol use, to change this divisiveness we need a revolution. It can happen with the miracle of love and nurture. There will need to be a visual change, that the average African Americans, that are trapped with these vices, they will need to see the progress of the African American Organization. And be willing to be rehabilitated, and seeing success in their community, friends and family change with this revolution.

The third level to climb is getting the average African American to believe in themselves to become stockholders and capitalists in the African American Organization. To stop being consumer slaves, and start identifying with what it means in their community to control their purchasing power, through owning the businesses we purchase from.

The average African American doesn't know; we have a trillion dollars' worth of purchasing power collectively. This power is given away to others from our consumer slave mentality, that permeates the average African American experience. The fourth level to climb is to put together social events and family meetings, where African Americans can come together bathe in our new found unity, and invest in our future, developing our wealth through the African American Organization capitalistic system.

Memorandum to the African Americans

The Solution

We have identified the problem as well as looking at our attitude. It's now time to speak on the solution and many may say, "the solution to what"? and I will reply; "to the poverty of the average African American." We know that African Americans have a trillion dollars in purchasing power. But what good will a trillion dollars in purchasing power do, when you can't harness it? This is where the challenge starts, when you have power and you're not aware of it, or you can't take advantage of it. Because of the lack of knowledge, and a plan to harness the power. This is where others can take advantage of us. *First, let's look at the power;*

> Because they're younger on average, black consumers are trendsetters and tastemakers for young consumers of all races, according to the Selig Center. They define mainstream culture and wield immense influence over how Americans choose to spend their money. Any marketing campaign targeting millennials "must include messages to reach African-American youth," notes Nielsen. Black buying power is projected to reach $1.2 trillion this year and $1.4 trillion by 2020, according to a report from the University of Georgia's Selig Center for Economic Growth. That's 275 percent growth since 1990, when black buying power was $320 billion. Already black consumers represent the largest consumers of color group in the marketplace, the report shows. (BOSCHMA, 2016)

This report of Selig Center shows African Americans are no more than consumer slaves, even though it seems to show African Americans have progressed financially. The problem is most African Americans don't really understand it, they just enjoy spending money without investing money. The buying power of African Americans is expected to grow even more. However, what is the return on the money we spend? We produce no products or services we just spend money.

While savvy marketers watch what young African Americans spend their money on. And from this they collect valuable information, to make a decision on advertising and marketing around the world. Young African Americans have style and creativity, many things they buy become trends, it's time to take advantage of this. In order for the average African Americans to participate in the development of the wealth plan. A change in attitude must take place, young African Americans

Memorandum to the African Americans

must come to the realization, that they must unite within an economical plan and become capitalists. This must consist of investment, production, training and customer service at the highest level of business, in and out of the African American businesses.

To produce these type of goals, I believe there must be an "African American Training Center." The center would be open to African Americans that are members of the African American Organization to develop capitalism. Professional African Americans will need to be recruited, to train young African-Americans to run these operations, that will be put in place. But more importantly, everyone that is a member of the organization must receive dividends, from profits that are generated from the several businesses the organization is engaged in. These dividends will be used to purchase the goods and services, that the organization will produce.

Our money must work for us, and not that we, just work for our money. Our money must circulate among us over and over again without leaving our grasp up to forty times. An inheritance must be left to the next generation, that is based on an economic business social order of capitalism, that is implement by the organization. Meaning a relationship with one another involves investing in ourselves, and the future of African-American children. Instead of always protesting, let's start investing, in order to change the outcome of our lifestyle.

Controlling our purchasing power and instituting capitalism within our ranks. We can put up the money need to elect our candidates and control the police department, instead of marching up and down the streets. We must be in a position to hire and fire, this is the type of system that African Americans need to put in place. So that the community will have the ability to control the money, that comes into our possession and run the community for our benefit. This can only happen when a plan is implemented with a strategy, which will involve making monetary sacrifices. We must be willing to risk capital in order to establish a solid foundation, for investment and return for profit.

By revealing this, don't think for one moment that the white man, isn't going find some way, to see if he can't stop us. He will be losing his consumer slaves and now you will be in competition with him. He'll research to see if we have broken any the laws, and he will send undercover black men to get near the leadership. And if he has to assassinate the leadership, it will be easier to do by sending undercover black men into the organization to do this. This why the leadership will

Memorandum to the African Americans

need security. If we start sending dividend checks or transferring funds in direct deposit to our members, he'll have the Security Exchange Commission, see if this is something they can do to stop this. This is why we must have or I's dotted and or t's cross every step of the way.

The first step would be like Harriet Tubman; we must go to the ghetto plantations to bring African Americans to economic freedom. The road to this economic freedom is dark and bumpy. Just like our ancestors were afraid when Harriet Tubman came to the plantations of the South, to take African Americans to freedom through the underground railroad.

Getting the African Americans today to leave the ghetto plantations, will be just as challenging as it was in those days. They will be afraid, that they will have to risk investing money, and uniting with their fellow African Americans nationwide. We need the average African Americans to think out the box. This will include being train in the development of capitalism and developing African American culture, that will allow this change to be successful.

Campaigning for African Americans to leave the ghetto plantations is no easy task. African Americans have never had economic freedom nationally; they will be in uncharted waters. This is dark and scary territory for them to travel, we must urge them on to economic freedom, keeping them focus so they won't turn back. As in the day of Harriet Tubman, we must let them know, there is risk involved and the danger of loss is possible. *These are the words of Harriet Tubman that relates to African Americans on the ghetto plantations:*

Harriet Tubman Quotes

"Every great dream begins with a dreamer. Always remember, you have within you the strength, the patience, and the passion to reach for the stars to change the world.
I freed a thousand slaves I could have freed a thousand more if only they knew they were slaves.
I grew up like a neglected weed - ignorant of liberty, having no experience of it.
Twant me, 'twas the Lord. I always told him, "I trust to you. I don't know where to go or what to do, but I expect you to lead me," and he always did."

The quotes of Harriet Tubman should open the eyes of understanding, of African Americans to realize the mission to get to the promised land of prosperity. That mission is to be a member of the African American Organization and become

Memorandum to the African Americans

a Stockholder and a Capitalist. This is the pathway to escape from the ghetto plantation and stop picking consumer cotton.

Step two as Brooker T. Washington founded the National Negro Business League he understood, that the African Americans need to be in business on a national scale. He went about making sure that African Americans were getting into businesses. *This is a report from the days when he started National Negro Business League:*

The League promoted the commercial endeavors and economic advancement of blacks mainly, but not solely in the South, via a network of state and local negro business leagues, and affiliated professional and trade organizations. Membership in the League was open to "any member of the race in good standing in his or her community," whether the person was in business, professional or private life. Meetings provided a forum in which African-American small businessmen shared stories of their struggles and successes.

Affiliated professional organizations included the National Negro Bankers Association, the National Negro Press Association, the National Association of Negro Funeral Directors, the National Negro Bar Association, the National Association of Negro Insurance Men, the National Negro Retail Merchants' Association, the National Association of Negro Real Estate Dealers, and the National Negro Finance Corporation.

I mostly agree with Brooker T. Washington forming a business league. However, there is no investment or inheritance component for a business, to continue producing profits for African Americans. The coming years after many of them pass away, they left no inheritance for the coming generations. One of the features of white people businesses they hand down their business to their children. There a terminology that is said, "this is old money" meaning they have been in business a long time through generations.

This is what needs to happen for the average African American to enjoy the wealth of this country. Through the generations that will come after us, that those that are in the membership of the organization. We will be able to leave and inheritance to our children and them to their grandchildren and so on. Our ancestors never got paid for the work, they did to build this country, or the promise kept, that they would receive forty acres and a mule. Andrew Johnson after the death of President Lincoln took away that promise from our ancestors.

Memorandum to the African Americans

The solution to our problem is leadership, our goal must be to united base on an economic relationship, that each African-American in the organization is a Stockholder and a Capitalist. We must have more than just a job, we need a partnership, ownership in the businesses, services and production of goods. Our production of these businesses will keep the money circulating in the organization and or communities.

Brooker T. Washington Quotes

Success is to be measured not so much by the position that one has reached in life as by the obstacles which he has overcome.

You can't hold a man down without staying down with him.

Few things can help an individual more than to place responsibility on him, and to let him know that you trust him.

I will permit no man to narrow and degrade my soul by making me hate him.

No race can prosper till it learns that there is as much dignity in tilling a field as in writing a poem.

Associate yourself with people of good quality, for it is better to be alone than in bad company.

There are two ways of exerting one's strength: one is pushing down, the other is pulling up.

If you want to lift yourself up, lift up someone else.

Character, not circumstances, makes the man.

Excellence is to do a common thing in an uncommon way.

These are lessons that have been left, but we must take it to the next level, with vision and creativity. So African Americans can escape to economic freedom instead on being consumer slaves, and pick consumer cotton, we must rebuild or leave the ghetto plantations.

The third step is, George Washington Carver, taught former slaves farming techniques for self-sufficiency; known for suggesting hundreds of uses for the peanut, and other plants. The vital information here is self-sufficiency, too many African Americans "single mothers" are on the welfare rolls. Too many African Americans lack education, George Washington Carver was and advocate for

Memorandum to the African Americans

learning how to do for yourself. In his day farming was a major way for African Americans to support themselves, without running to the white man for a handout.

There is a saying "give a man a fish and you'll feed him for a day. But teach a man to fish and he can eat for a lifetime." We must teach the average African Americans how to fish.

I see this as coming together as a family, to deal with family problems within the African American community and our lineage. There must be self-determination to make the plan of investing in ourselves work. George Washington Carver further teaches us that we need to produce things out of what we have available. He made products out of peanuts and plants, with study and experimenting, something that is a great method to uncover unique possibilities. This must be implemented in the plan for investing and profit for African Americans in the organization.

George Washington Carver Quotes

Education is the key to unlock the golden door of freedom.

When you do the common things in life in an uncommon way, you will command the attention of the world.

Ninety-nine percent of the failures come from people who have the habit of making excuses.

Fear of something is at the root of hate for others, and hate within will eventually destroy the hater.

I love to think of nature as an unlimited broadcasting station, through which God speaks to us every hour, if we will only tune in.

Where there is no vision, there is no hope.

Learn to do common things uncommonly well; we must always keep in mind that anything that helps fill the dinner pail is valuable.

Since new developments are the products of a creative mind, we must therefore stimulate and encourage that type of mind in every way possible.

There is no short cut to achievement. Life requires thorough preparation - veneer isn't worth anything.

Memorandum to the African Americans

Self-determination will bring the African American today into the future and to the field of prosperity, were the fruit of our labor will be rewarded, with the joy of accomplishment. It's time to stand up to reality and embrace our destiny. Self-determination must not be feared, but receive with open arms.

The fourth step is, looking at the Honorable Elijah Muhammad, let me tell you what he teaches us. I grew up in Boston, Massachusetts, there was a friend of mine named Steve Nelson, said to me "let's go to the Muslims meeting of The Nation of Islam." I agreed, we went to Mosque 11 on Intervale Street. To go in we had to be searched, and then we were led to our seats by the usher.

The minister at the time was Louis Farrakhan, two guards stood erect in front of him as he spoke. As Louis Farrakhan preach, the teachings of the Honorable Elijah Muhammad, and that the white man is a devil. After the meeting, I was very impressed with the orderly service, and how clean shaven and well dress all the men were, and the security they afford the leadership.

I never became a Muslim; I believe in Yahuwah the Messiah also known as Jesus Christ. Yet, I have the deepest respect for the organization, discipline, security and the dress code of the Nation of Islam. I would adopt these elements into any national organization that I would establish. In Boston, I would go to Grove Hall, where many of the Nation of Islam businesses were located.

I would frequent the restaurants, and I love the bean pies they would sell. But what most impress me, is that many African American men released from prison, that went into the Nation of Islam, were clean up and given purpose. One of the best examples is Malcom Little who became Malcom X after he was released from prison. Elijah Muhammad allowed him to develop into a national figure through the Nation of Islam.

The sadness of the relationship is they separated on very bad terms. The white man (FBI J Edgar Hoover) use this to his advantage. By sending inflammatory letters of lies to Elijah Muhammad signed by Malcom X, this help, set up Malcom X to be assassinated. The Black man must respect each other and if there are differences between us they must be settled with dignity, and never air dirty laundry in public. I believe that Malcom X should have left the Nation of Islam without speaking a word against Elijah Muhammad, Elijah Muhammad made Malcom X a national figure through the Nation of Islam. Even though Malcom X felt that Elijah Muhammad father children. Malcom X should have never said a

Memorandum to the African Americans

word of it publicly and left the Nation of Islam quietly. He fell into the trap of blacks fighting among themselves.

The Honorable Elijah Muhammad didn't murder anyone. and there was no reason for Malcom X to run and tell the white man, it was the Nation of Islam private business. Malcom X confronted Elijah Muhammad after that he should have walked away quietly, this is my personal opinion. The significant lessons I would take from The Honorable Elijah Muhammad the messenger of Allah is organization, discipline, security at public and private events, clean businesses and a proper dress code.

The Honorable Elijah Muhammad Quotes

"You and I may go to Harvard, we may go to York of England, or go to Al Ahzar in Cairo and get degrees from all of these great seats of learning. But we will never be recognized until we recognize our women."

— Elijah Muhammad, Message to the Blackman in America

"No nation will ever respect us as long as we beg for that which we can do for ourselves. There has never been a leader of our people who went all-out to set up an economic plan for our people. I use the saying of Jesus, "All before me were thieves and robbers.""

— Elijah Muhammad, Message to the Blackman in America

"Don't condemn if you see a person has a dirty glass of water, just show them the clean glass of water that you have. When they inspect it, you won't have to say that yours is better."

— Elijah Muhammad

I respect the leadership of The Honorable Elijah Muhammad however; I believe that religion has no place in the economic development of capitalism. Religion is something that is a personal choice outside of the organization standards. A person can be in any religion one desire, as long as it doesn't conflict with the mission of developing wealth for African Americans. I believe one should have the right do whatever you want as long as it doesn't break the laws of the United States and the States we live in. I believe in God and I trust God, but there

Memorandum to the African Americans

should be no struggle of theology, as we work to develop the commonwealth of African Americans, religion can easily get in the way.

The fifth step is, Martin Luther King Jr. who was the President of Southern Christian Leadership Conference (SCLC) He stood up to the white racism of America. He parted the sea of white racism, and walk on the dry land of civil rights, leading African Americans to the shore of freedom. He was highly educated with a PH.D. in theology. He shouldered the burden of the civil rights movement, taking beatings, going to jail and ultimately becoming a martyr. Martin Luther King Jr. expounded nonviolent and march for civil rights, voting rights, jobs, and integration. With the "March on Washington" he delivered the "I have a Dream" speech and also put together the Poor People's Campaign:

> The Poor People's Campaign was motivated by a desire for economic justice: the idea that all people should have what they need to live. King and the SCLC shifted their focus to these issues after observing that gains in civil rights had not improved the material conditions of life for many African Americans (Wikipedia, 1968)

Martin Luther King Jr. did a lot by marching and protesting, but he came to realize, that there was no economic gain, from all the protesting and marching for civil rights. Martin Luther King Jr. then believed it was time to beg the white man for jobs and economic justice. Through the Poor People Campaign, well the economic justice hasn't happened even until this day. There is a need for African Americans to put together and economic plan.

We need to develop wealth instead of begging the white man for the crumbs that falls off his table. This is something that Martin Luther King Jr. never identify, as he worked tirelessly to uplift the poor in this nation. This has been a flaw with many of our African American leaders. They never put an economic plan, with residual income, self- determination to rid poverty among African Americans, and economic inheritance for the coming generations. Martin Luther King Jr. didn't believe in capitalism, He wrote a letter to his wife and said,

> "I imagine you already know that I am much more socialistic in my economic theory than capitalistic… [Capitalism] started out with a noble and high motive… but like most human systems it fell victim to the very thing it was revolting against. So today capitalism has out-lived its usefulness." – Letter to Coretta Scott, July 18, 1952.

Memorandum to the African Americans

And one day we must ask the question, 'Why are there forty million poor people in America? And when you begin to ask that question, you are raising questions about the economic system, about a broader distribution of wealth.' When you ask that question, you begin to question the capitalistic economy. And I'm simply saying that more and more, we've got to begin to ask questions about the whole society..." –Speech to Southern Christian Leadership Conference Atlanta, Georgia, August 16, 1967. (HALPER, 2016)

Martin Luther King Jr. had a very anti-capitalistic view, I believe this has held African Americans back. Socialist views don't cover the capital (money) needed to operate in the capitalist society. When Martin in 1955-1956 instituted Montgomery bus boycott, it hit the bus owner's capital, and made them change their policies, they saw that they were losing capital. They took African Americans to court but capitalism won out. So, "King said of the bus boycott: ''We came to see that, in the long run, it is more honorable to walk in dignity than ride in humiliation."

The white bus owner allowed African Americans, to set anywhere on the bus as long as, they paid their money to ride the bus. To me this shows that controlling our money power we can set anywhere we want on the economic bus. However, the African American Organization, we don't want to just ride the bus, we want African Americans to own their bus and bus system. Capitalism has been accepted around the world even in communist countries breaking down the barriers of communism to accept capitalism. Morality got in the way of Martin Luther King Jr. thinking that capitalism is evil. I believe it can be good or evil, it depends on the people that operate the system of capitalism. We cannot get away from capitalism; Martin Luther King Jr. wrote to his wife in 1952 that "capitalism has out-lived its usefulness."

Well! Sixty-four years after that letter, capitalism is very strong and its time for African Americans to embrace it. Capitalism can build wealth in the African American community.

Martin Luther King Jr. Quotes

Darkness cannot drive out darkness; only light can do that. Hate cannot drive out hate; only love can do that.

Life's most persistent and urgent question is, 'What are you doing for others?

Memorandum to the African Americans

Nothing in all the world is more dangerous than sincere ignorance and conscientious stupidity.

The time is always right to do what is right.

I have decided to stick with love. Hate is too great a burden to bear.

The ultimate measure of a man is not where he stands in moments of comfort and convenience, but where he stands at times of challenge and controversy.

Our lives begin to end the day we become silent about things that matter.

Faith is taking the first step even when you don't see the whole staircase.

Injustice anywhere is a threat to justice everywhere.

We must accept finite disappointment, but never lose infinite hope.

The lesson I have learned from Martin Luther King Jr. we must keep a positive attitude and to be ready to stand up to racism. With education, nonviolent, and the power of love. We must also be willing to work with all people for the good of America, and the human race.

The sixth step is, Malcom X became El-Hajj Malik El-Shabazz after leaving the Nation of Islam. He also became one of the founders of the Organization of Afro-America Unity. Malcom X came to realize how essential African American unity was to changing the lives of African Americans. He wrote "The Basic Unity Program." This program called for Restoration, Reorientation, Education, Economic Security, and Self-Defense as a means of promoting Pan-African unity and interests. ***These are some the statements Malcom X made:***

Writings from The Basic Unity Program

After enslaving us, the slave masters developed a racist educational system which justified to its posterity the evil deeds that had been committed against the African people and their descendants. Too often the slave himself participates so completely in this system that he justifies having been enslaved and oppressed.

After the Emancipation Proclamation, when the system of slavery changed from chattel slavery to wage slavery, it was realized that the Afro-

Memorandum to the African Americans

American constituted the largest homogeneous ethnic group with a common origin and common group experience in the United States and, if allowed to exercise economic or political freedom, would in a short period of time own this country. Therefore, racists in this government developed techniques that would keep the Afro-American people economically dependent upon the slave masters -- economically slaves -- twentieth-century slaves.

Understanding that our struggle is part of a larger world struggle of oppressed peoples against all forms of oppression. We must change the thinking of the Afro-American by liberating our minds through the study of philosophies and psychologies, cultures and languages that did not come from our racist oppressors. (El-Shabazz, 1965).

Malcom X was ready to become a major player on the world stage, to turn darkness into light, in the world of the African Americans. He came to the revelation that unity would lift African Americans out of poverty, and remove them from the oppression of the white man. If you read "The Basic Unity Program" that he wanted to implement. You will see the attitude he wanted to establish nationwide and worldwide. The leadership he would have provided, would have made a significant change in African American development.

He was gun down by the Nation of Islam, and I believe sanction by the FBI on February 21, 1965. The problem was he decided not to have a search for weapons, basically setting himself up to be a martyr. So his family would no longer be in danger, they had bombed his house a week earlier. There was no one that could take his place in the "Organization of Afro-America Unity."

I have learned from Malcom X that African American Unity is the highest priority. Don't forget Mother Africa, be ready to do a brisk business with the continent. And that an African American leader of his stature should be protected at all times, with the highest of security standards.

Malcom X A.K.A El-Hajj Malik El-Shabazz Quotes

You can't separate peace from freedom because no one can be at peace unless he has his freedom.

Education is the passport to the future, for tomorrow belongs to those who prepare for it today.

If you don't stand for something you will fall for anything.

Memorandum to the African Americans

Be peaceful, be courteous, obey the law, respect everyone; but if someone puts his hand on you, send him to the cemetery.

Usually when people are sad, they don't do anything. They just cry over their condition. But when they get angry, they bring about a change.

You're not to be so blind with patriotism that you can't face reality. Wrong is wrong, no matter who does it or says it.

Without education, you are not going anywhere in this world.

Truth is on the side of the oppressed.

If you're not ready to die for it, put the word 'freedom' out of your vocabulary.

I believe in human beings, and that all human beings should be respected as such, regardless of their color.

Malcom X at least had a plan of unity, I would suggest to the reader to read his "The Basic Unity Program" there is a great deal I agree with. However, it doesn't have a wealth developing component for the average African American to pass profits (inheritance) on to the next generation. But it does have some instructions that African Americans should follow. Instructions I seek to contrivance into the organization.

Economic unity is the key for the average African American to move out of poverty. Without unity it just won't work, because of all the roadblocks to success, that have been set up by the white man for the average African American to make sure we fail. The power of unity makes us stronger than we would be alone. Unity creates more opportunities for the spectrum of African Americans. The challenge is to bring the average African American together for developing commonwealth and money power. This is something we must explore and accomplish for ourselves and the next generation. It's time to talk about Money Power.

Money Power

The seventh step is, The African American Organization we seek to unite the average African American on the basis of money power. African Americans have a trillion dollars in money power. The Average African American is a consumer slave, but doesn't understand this our even care, we spend our money on products and services. Accumulating things in our lives that will soon deteriorate and

Memorandum to the African Americans

depreciate. The money we spend will not circulate back to us. The system of consumer slavery is set up as a trap for the average African American, to send our wealth into the hands of others and keep us on the ghetto plantation while picking consumer cotton.

This means we as a people don't accumulate capital and this is why our communities are run down. We have no capital to change the landscape, we as a people are capital less rather than capitalist. Our leaders have always been focusing on getting something, from the white man through protesting and marching. As Martin Luther King Jr. and Malcom X discover. This method has left the African Americans in poverty. We have civil rights, voting rights and this has put a Black President in the White House. But the Average African-American is still in poverty.

The struggle for freedom was mostly base on political strategy. Brooker T Washington wanted to have African Americans obtain freedom base on economic power. But there was no unity in his plan to control money power for the coming generations. The business league he built up for black businesses didn't leave an inheritance for the coming generations. Money power has been ignored by African American leaders, let's talk about money power. Let me start by discussing this, "America use capitalism which means; an economic and political system in which a country's trade and industry are controlled by private owners for profit, rather than by the state." *Let's speak to the history of capitalism:*

> **The history of capitalism can be traced back to early forms of merchant capitalism practiced in Western Europe during the Middle Ages. It began to develop into its modern form during the Early Modern period in the Protestant countries of North-Western Europe, especially the Netherlands and England. Traders in Amsterdam and London created the first chartered joint-stock companies driving up commerce and trade, and the first stock exchanges and banking and insurance institutions were established**

> **Over the course of the past five hundred years, capital has been accumulated by a variety of different methods, in a variety of scales, and associated with a great deal of variation in the concentration of economic power and wealth. Much of the history of the past five hundred years is concerned with the development of capitalism in its various forms.** (Wikipedia, 2016)

Memorandum to the African Americans

Europeans created capitalism just as the Europeans came to America and started modern slavery. Developing enormous wealth, and control over of the world's commerce, producing trade in Europe, Africa, and America. Europe has sucked up the world wealth for the past five hundred years. In the new land of America and with the system of slavery the Europeans made America a world power. The generations of Europeans born in America broke away from the tyranny of British rule and produce the Constitution.

African Americans for decades had to fight the tyranny of European white racism. African American leaders use the Constitution to fight white racism in the courts of this nation. While fighting for freedom they neglected capitalism. Capitalism to African Americans is like curse word link to dirty work. African Americans have never really try to harness capitalism through unity as one people. Working to develop commonwealth as a goal, this leads me to money power.

Money has a negative connotation for the average African American, it something many has never had much of. Many quote the saying "money is the root of all evil" but the complete quote is" the love of money is the root of all evil" and the need of money can become evil too. But it hard constantly struggling to survive in a white racist wealthy country. Understanding nothing about money power that white people grew up for hundreds of years, using the system of capitalism. The cry for freedom, justice, and equality is what the young African Americans heard morning, noon and night. Seeing the injustice, the oppression, and murder of African Americans.

African Americans have seen so much white racism, wherever we travel in this country. How then could our leaders focus on money power, it was always the intention of the white authority, to make sure that African Americans are economical, deaf, dumb and blind to capitalism. And to make sure capital is not available to African Americans and most of all their communities, thus the ghetto plantations. The white man wants to make sure African Americans don't understand how to use the capital to their advantage. This would also make sure you can't secure loans because you will have no collateral to back a loan. Basically, the African American is capital less and money starved, so you can be relegated to poverty.

The banking system created by the Europeans formulate the platform, for capital that has stood for centuries, throughout the global economy, even until this today. The banking system, is a well-oiled machine in America, through the

Memorandum to the African Americans

Federal Reserve, that issues money and interest rates. To the average African American this is purely meaningless, only because we have always had an immediate need for money. Therefore, diluting our possible strength, in controlling money power, within the African- American community, so we have no desire to invest in ourselves.

I have outlined the problem; the challenge becomes how can we wake up the average African American. And demonstrate to them how to control a trillion dollars in money power that are in the hands of African-Americans. Along with controlling money power, it will benefit themselves, their children and their children, children. I submit to you it can be done; first I will offer membership into the "African American Organization" for an African American to become a member you must be willing pay a hundred-dollar non-refundable entry fee. This membership gives the African American a membership account, access to private membership information and the business plan. The business plan is about investment, training, social events, products and services development.

The African American Organization will insist that every member must also send another hundred dollars and place up to thousand dollars into your membership account. For the purpose of investing in the products, services, and training, that will be developed at the African American training center. We request that members place at least a thousand dollar in the account in this initial stage of the development of the African American Organization, this is for investment purpose only. This is the maximum you can put in the account; no member can put no more, than a thousand dollars into the account; this will give a level playing field for all our members when distributing dividends.

It is also to make sure every member is a Stockholder and a Capitalist; with the products or services, we have produced. There is major information about this operation, that will be available to members only. And all the "standard operating procedures" will not be explained in this book. Know this, there will be legal ramifications, that must be handled by the legal department, for Security Exchange Commission (SEC) that regulates stock and dividends. We must be concerned that tax evasions laws aren't broken, the white man would love to send the leadership to jail.

Don't think that the white man is just going to let his consumer slaves walk away from the ghetto plantations, he has always kept them on; and stop them from picking consumer cotton? But just like Harriet Tubman who went back to the

Memorandum to the African Americans

plantation to free our ancestors. We must be willing to take the risk of investing in ourselves to have economic freedom, by developing money power among ourselves. There will be products and services coming out of the "African American Training Center," production and service teams will be formed from the membership and committees. The committees will approve products and services for investments to be brought to the marketplace. The "African American Organization" will need millions of average African Americans to be members of the organization and to participate in all the committees, operations, and functions.

The "African American Training Center" is for members of the "African American Organization" members will be trained in all aspects of the organization, investment, businesses, events, technology and etiquette. In the training center education will be a high priority, the "African American Training Center" will be used for instruction in controlling money power. Teachers, students, and teams will be developing products and services; this is the goal of the training center. The goal will also be to produce jobs, that African Americans will be employed in. Within these businesses, our top priority must be an impeccable treatment of customers. Also high-class top-notch customer service, with well manner staff showing good etiquette, very clean establishments, and proper dress code. This will be for the general public to enjoy doing business with our businesses.

Family meetings will be put together to recruit the average African American. Our hope is that we can get African American celebrities, involved in these social events. African Americans will always have high unemployment, because of racism. But the money that Africans Americans accumulate and control, for investment purposes along with this capitalistic system, will lower unemployment among African Americans. Too many average African Americans will think this is impossible; because of and uncertainty of mistrust among African Americans since slavery.

The major concern will be there is no way, an investment can be made with small money; small money can add up to big money. The fact is that we have to start somewhere and it must be among ourselves, this is where becoming a capitalist plays a major role. That is why controlling money power has to be understood, and accumulating capital gives us the economic power to do powerful things. It has been so many times that white politician meets with African American leaders. Too beg white business owners to hire African Americans for jobs. I don't blame white people for our high unemployment.

Memorandum to the African Americans

I blame the average African American; for the lack of economic unity. I will say this, "that the leadership hasn't been available", but it is now here with "Memorandum to the African Americans". Understand this, once the average African American gives the white businesses competition. And the average African American control their money power. White business owners will want to start and investigation and surveillance, into our business practices. This is where we must be "wise as a serpent and gentle as a dove."

Money Power is the operation of capitalism for the purpose of developing wealth among the average African American, yet there will be the fear of loss, and the potential is there. **Malcom X said, "If you don't stand for something you will fall for anything."** We must unite and control or money power so we can stop living like consumer slaves. So we won't have to beg the white man for jobs. **Brooker T Washington said, "Success is to be measured not so much by the position that one has reached in life, as by the obstacles which he has overcome."** The obstacles in the way of the average African American is fear, addiction, easily manipulated, by advertisement and the television. It will be a challenge to release them from this hypnotic illusion. **Martin Luther King Jr. said, "Nothing in all the world is more dangerous than sincere ignorance and conscientious stupidity."** There is a great deal of sincere ignorance and conscientious stupidity in the ranks of the average African American, when it comes to understanding capitalism, this needs to change immediately. **Harriet Tubman said, "I freed a thousand slaves I could have freed a thousand more if only they knew they were slaves."** The average African American doesn't know he or she is a consumer slave, so it will be hard to get them to leave slave thinking, and the ghetto plantation and many of them love picking consumer cotton, leaving no inheritance for their children.

We must lift ourselves up by our own bootstraps. And stop looking to others to help us, we need to help ourselves. We must fight the good fight of faith, by taking a chance on each other even if it is at great risk, which can bring great rewards. Even though fear of loss or failure stands at the door of our destiny, these attributes will do nothing, but keep us back from success.

I have written "Memorandum to the African Americans" in the greatest hope that It will start an economic revolution. "I have a revelation" that the average African American can enjoy wealth in this country through, unity in the "African American Organization." Understanding money power and becoming a

Memorandum to the African Americans

Stockholder and a Capitalist. And working on how to control this money power for the commonwealth of the average African American. Let it be said, "Arise, Black man, and Black woman take your rightful place in history, don't be afraid of the darkness, for the light is within you."

Mastering the Capitalist System

Capitalism is an economic system based on private ownership of the means of production and their operation for profit. Characteristics central to capitalism include private property, capital accumulation, wage labor, voluntary exchange, a price system, and competitive markets. (Wikipedia, 2016)

I believe this needs to be reiterated, my mission in this revelation is to get the average African American to become a member of the African American Organization, then a Stockholder and a Capitalist. In profit motive, this is where you find out the real mechanics of capitalism.

THE PROFIT MOTIVE

In capitalism, the motive for producing goods and services is to sell them for a profit, not to satisfy people's needs. The products of capitalist production have to find a buyer, of course, but this is only incidental to the main aim of making a profit, of ending up with more money than was originally invested. This is not a theory that we have thought up but a fact you can easily confirm for yourself by reading the financial press. Production is started not by what consumers are prepared to pay for to satisfy their needs, but by what the capitalists calculate can be sold at a profit. Those goods may satisfy human needs but those needs will not be met if people do not have sufficient money.

The profit motive is not just the result of greed on behalf of individual capitalists. They do not have a choice about it. The need to make a profit is imposed on capitalists as a condition for not losing their investments and their position as capitalists. Competition with other capitalists forces them to reinvest as much of their profits as they can afford to keep their means and methods of production up to date. (World Socialist Movement, 2016)

Memorandum to the African Americans

Most African Americans don't have knowledge or even and inclination about capitalism. How it runs our lives and how the system determines our future. From the cradle we are affected by capitalism, it would behoove us to understand it workings, and to master it, to benefit our lives. Let this be repeated; "Capitalism is an economic system based on private ownership of the means of production and their operation for profit."

The African American Organization will open training centers for this purpose. The membership will be involved in private stock holdings, a capitalistic economic system, that produce goods and services for a profit. Members will share in the profit; from this form of capitalism, a dividend will be issued to the members. Money power will be the basis to create, and operate the African American Organization businesses and services. There must be an accumulation of capital from the membership, this is to set a pattern of understanding, we need to invest in ourselves, we will not ask for loans from the white man.

Let me say this for the record; I would like to be wealthy, but not without making many other African Americans wealthy, from a child this has been within me. I believe that God called me to be a leader of African Americans. I want to get millions upon millions of African Americans to follow me, in the African American Organization. I would lead them to the crops of capitalism to harvest the money power, that is in their own hands. I would not beg the white man for anything, but I would request African Americans to invest in themselves. To control the products, services and businesses that African American Organization, will produce as African Americans did in 1921 which was called Black Wall Street.

A portion of the profits would be distributed to members through a dividend. The dividend money distributed to members is to be saved, reinvested or spent back on our products, services and businesses that African American Organization controls and owns, so we can recycle our capital (money). This is the basis of our capitalist system within the African American Organization. We can then build the commonwealth for average African American, we must become Stockholders and Capitalists.

To get the average African American to understand this method, of mastering the capitalist system, is just like Harriet Tubman went to the plantations in the days of slavery. Trying to get the African Americans in though days to escape and go the North were African Americans can be free. There was a great fear of the white

Memorandum to the African Americans

man, and the doubt of the competency of those that were trying to get the slaves to leave the plantation.

When asking the average African American to invest in themselves they will say, "I have no money to invest", of course, it takes sacrifice to invest in yourself. If you had to collect cans and save the money to invest, to become a member of African American Organization, then that is what needs to happen to master this capitalistic system.

Our ancestors that left the plantations of the South. I'm sure they were afraid, that they would be caught by the white man and punished for trying to escape. This same type of fear and mistrust will undoubtedly happen with the average African American. Asking, what can my little money power do? How can this capitalistic system change the economic future of African Americans?

We have been consumer slaves for so long, that the slave mentality has infected or thinking to such a degree we are hypnotized. Asking the average African American to escape from the ghetto plantation and stop picking consumer cotton, is unthinkable to the average African American. The chains of poverty are wrap around their minds, and their puppet strings are pulled by the white man's advertisement.

The African American Organization strategy is to bring the average African Americans into the training center, social events, and to show them the value of becoming a member. Also helping them to understand how to control the money power and execute the capitalistic system that has been set up. We must set up our accumulation capital (Banks), own private property, wage labor, voluntary exchange, a price system, and competitive markets.

For the record many will say, "isn't this discrimination, to focus only on African Americans." I will reply; "This is a family problem within my family, slavery was perpetrated on African Americans. We haven't recovered from this brutal and Godless application of dehumanizing African Americans, even until this day. This is my family and I have the right to develop procedures, that will help us overcome the devastating effects, that slavery has had on African Americans."

There is something I want to bring to light in writing "Memorandum to the African Americans." In 1964 President Lyndon B. Johnson declared the Economic Opportunity Act (EOA) would launch the "war on poverty." Well, poverty is still here decades later, there have been many other programs, that have tried to deal

Memorandum to the African Americans

with poverty in America. The war on poverty has been no more than giving handouts to the poor. So African Americans wouldn't unite and use capitalism to develop wealth.

It still comes down to, "give a man a fish and he will eat for a day. But teach a man how to fish and he will eat for life." No matter how many programs the government has devised, it will not stop poverty, through handouts. The attitude (thinking) of African Americans has to be changed. It's not about having money, it's the way we think, and use the money we have, so we can develop wealth in a capitalistic society. If you gave a million dollars to a poor person, most likely that person will soon have no money or very little money left. They would start spending right away, never thinking about investing it.

But if you teach a poor person how to make a million dollars through capitalism, that person would no longer be poor because of the education that helps, them to get a million dollars. Because they work for it and made a profit, and learn the system, they would probably make more. There is over forty million African Americans in America, there is still a great deal of poverty among us in the riches country in the world, there is something inherently wrong. But the fact is we have no capitalistic system among ourselves, and without training the white man will take every dime we generate.

The African American Organization isn't out to give away money. Neither or we telling the average African American, that this is some kind of get rich, quick scheme, or a Ponzi scheme. Money power and mastering the capitalistic system, we advocate will take time and sacrifice. It's like building a building, you must first put the plan together, and then prepare to lay a solid foundation to build upon. Our first order of business is accumulation and ownership of capital. While making all the members of the African American Organization into Stockholders and Capitalists.

Next, our members are to participate in creating the businesses, working in the businesses, producing products and services, of the African American Organization through teamwork. As a reward in time, receive a dividend, also receive a salary for those that work in the operations. Over a period of time, this will take the average African American out of poverty, by the accumulation and ownership of capital, generating wealth, also the ability to leave an inheritance for the next generation.

Memorandum to the African Americans

The African American Organization is targeting twenty-five million African-Americans to become members, to control our money power, then it will be no problem, we can then take advantage of capitalism, capitalize products, services, and goals of investments. Of course millions of African Americans or under the hypnotic illusion of the white man, and trapped on ghetto plantations and are gladly picking consumer cotton.

They're being bound to live in the condition they do because they have no choice or vision. When true leadership comes, the white man is going to work to stop African Americans from unifying. Just as Confederates in the South didn't want to free the slaves. And build a system after the Civil war, the Emancipation Proclamation, and Reconstruction to entrap African Americans in a Jim Crow system. Where white Southerners in acted laws that would deny African Americans any rights to the American Dream.

You must realize that an enormous amount of people make a good living off the ignorance and the disunity of African Americans. Our poverty and consumer slavery feeds this country's elite, politicians and immigrants. Organizing African Americans to united, love and respect themselves as a people, and instill the control of money power and mastering the capitalist system, would make such a change. That many would first criticize, then try to become a part of us, then imitate what, we have done. Just like many imitate the music and fashions we created and others receive the lion share of the profits of our creations. It is important that without a doubt, we must master this capitalistic system.

Our Future

To clearly step into the future, we must be aware of what is taking place now. We no longer live in the industrial age; we live in the technological age. In order to benefit in the technology age, we must learn the technology that surrounds our life. Computers are global, they are based on science, math, engineering, and physics. A scientific education needs to be given to young African Americans to compete in the world today. The African American Organization will open training centers in order to educate young African Americans in software development, networking, cyber security and all aspect of technology, plus product development, services, and apps.

Memorandum to the African Americans

This also is a pathway out of poverty, and a building block to ensure a prosperous future. The industrialist built America, on the back of slaves, and the global markets. The industrialist white man also perpetrated racism all over the world. The generation of industrialist white men are dying off, and institutionalize racism is becoming the new norm. African Americans must forge a new era with unity and the control of money power, through mastering this capitalistic system. African Americans must become capitalist, and operate this system in order to take advantage of the ever-changing technology that is coming to light. Soon there will be quantum computers coming to the marketplace.

We need young African Americans learning the technology and playing a major role in getting these computers to market. The key to the future is, we must always keep our fingers on the pulse of the economy. We will need to adjust our capitalistic system to meet the needs of the market so that the coming generation can continue to make profits.

While also allowing the creativity of the next generation to express itself. Looking into the future and preparing for it takes insight, the type of insight that has to be free from the slave mentality. Also, critical thinking must be applied every step of the way; meaning an analysis of our members and the system being use must be evaluated. To see what results are being produced and adjust it for the next generation to keep benefiting. This is to make sure they will be able to continue to progress and stay out of the prison of poverty.

The future that is being layout in the "Memorandum to the African Americans" can only come to fruition. Through Middle-class African Americans stepping into the revolution and working to execute the revelation. While reaching out to understand how to reach back to our family members, friends, and bring them into the capitalistic system with nurturing and patience. African Americans that are low income and uneducated have the brutal scars of consumer slavery, police harassment, judicial entrapment, and bureaucracy red tape for welfare and government services, they must be reprogramed. There are drugs dealer, drug addicts, gangs, pimps, prostitution, and other vices that have grip the minds of African Americans on the ghetto plantations.

It is vital that we remove the community of these vices, only through an actual display that the capitalistic system is working. African American Organization members will have income that they aren't working for to show the family and friends that the capitalist system works. And the average African American can be

Memorandum to the African Americans

a part of this process. By turning away from the vices and turning to a capitalistic system that brings success to our community and our future.

The future is what we make of it today. If you have read the "Memorandum to the African Americans" this far and your African American. You have made an amazing accomplishment, now the eyes of your understanding should be open. The fundamental question is will you become a member of the African American Organization and help others to see the light?

Memorandum to the African Americans

Membership

To all members, there is a one-time hundred-dollar non-refundable entry fee. A hundred-dollar will need, to be placed into your membership account to start with. The non-refundable fee is for processing your membership so you can receive a certificate of membership, ID number, and information for members only, also putting your name in the organization database, so you can be invited to meetings, events, and webinars.

You must at least have a hundred dollars in your account, you will also need to bring your membership account up to a thousand dollars. Funding your account is for the purpose of investment, producing products, services and to produce a profit to distribute a dividend. All members will be a Stockholder in the African American Organization, this is to lay the foundation for mastering the capitalistic system. No stock will be issued until product, services are approved, and all legal terms are completely layout and fulfilled.

The African American Organization is requesting that all members place at least one thousand dollars into their membership account, this is the maximum you can place into the account and no more. The reason for this is to level the playing field when distributing dividends. Information will be sent to you, to work through issues as we lay a foundation for developing the commonwealth among African Americans. You may be thinking will two hundred to a thousand dollars build the foundation. Yes, it will take millions of African Americans participating in this process, this is the first step in a thousand-mile journey.

You also need to fill out an application showing your education, and any skills you have acquired; this will be placed in the database. You must be eighteen or older to submit an application. It's also a requirement that anyone considering becoming a member must first read the book, "Memorandum to the African Americans." You can submit your application at www.africanamericanorg.com, you can also email us at africanameriorg@outlook.com to be considered for various positions that will need to be filled. The African American Organization needs recruiters, which is a paid commission job. Also, we want African Americans that have a bloodline to descendants of slaves in America. These are our ancestors that were treated inhumanely, we are their descendants. So we can

Memorandum to the African Americans

honor their memory and lift up our heritage, we are thankful for them, living through the brutal, Godless, torture of slavery.

We are thankful for their courage to live in a white racist Nation, that denied them their human rights. It's time for us to guide the future generations with economic unity, respect, honor, discipline and love that they were never afforded. Our relationship will be based on capitalism and honor as we forge into this new frontier. I Brother Saul, would like to make millionaires out of mostly all the members of the African American Organization. I know and believe this can be done, if the average African Americans, will let go of the vices, and train to stop being brain-washed. We must snap out of the hypnotic illusion of the white man, so we can accomplish being wealthy as a people.

In conclusion, the only barrier that can hold us back is unbelief, and intentionally blinding ourselves to the fact, we possess a great deal of money power. Also, fearing we don't have the knowledge or the determination to pursue the course that is set before us, the course of being a Stockholder and a Capitalist. Let it be said again, "Arise, Black man, and Black woman take your rightful place in history, don't be afraid of the darkness, for the light is within you."

Go to www.pbs.com and watch "Slavery by another Name"
also "Many Rivers to Cross" These documentaries show the history of African Americans something you should know.

Website: africanamericanorg.com
Email: africanameriorg@outlook.com

Photo credit: slaveryinamerica.tumblr.com

Memorandum to the African Americans

References

BLACK DEMOGRAPHIC NEWS. (2014, June 12). *Poverty in Black America.* Retrieved from BLACKDEMOGRAPHICS.com : http://blackdemographics.com/households/poverty/

BOSCHMA, J. (2016, February 2). *Black Consumers Have 'Unprecedented Impact'.* Retrieved from The Atlantic: http://www.theatlantic.com/politics/archive/2016/02/black-consumers-have-unprecedented-impact-in-2015/433725/

Drug Policy Alliance. (2016, June 14). *Race and the Drug War.* Retrieved from Drug Policy Alliance: http://www.drugpolicy.org/race-and-drug-war

El-Shabazz, E.-H. M. (1965, February 15). *Malcom-X.* Retrieved from Malcom X: http://www.malcolm-x.org/docs/gen_oaau.htm

Farbota, K. (2015, September 2). *Black Crime Rates: What Happens When Numbers Aren't Neutral.* Retrieved from The Huffington Post: http://www.huffingtonpost.com/kim-farbota/black-crime-rates-your-st_b_8078586.html

Haley, A. (2016, June 17). *Autobiograhpy of Malcom X.* Retrieved from al-rasid.com: http://al-rasid.com/shared_uploads/The.Autobiography.of.MalcolmX.pdf

HALPER, K. (2016, January 11). *11 Most Anti-Capitalist Quotes from Martin Luther King, Jr.* Retrieved from rawstory: http://www.rawstory.com/2016/01/11-most-anti-capitalist-quotes-from-martin-luther-king-jr/

Lynch, W. (1712, December 25). *Internet Archive.* Retrieved from Internet Archive: https://archive.org/stream/WillieLynchLetter1712/the_willie_lynch_letter_the_making_of_a_slave_1712_djvu.txt

NAACP. (2015, June 12). *CRIMINAL JUSTICE FACT SHEET.* Retrieved from NAACP: http://www.naacp.org/pages/criminal-justice-fact-sheet

Simkin, J. (2016, June 12). *Lynching.* Retrieved from Spartacus Educational: http://spartacus-educational.com/USAlynching.htm

Wikipedia. (1968, May 12). *Poor People's Campaign.* Retrieved from Wikipedia: https://en.wikipedia.org/wiki/Poor_People%27s_Campaign

Wikipedia. (2016, June 21). *Capitalism.* Retrieved from Wikipedia: https://en.wikipedia.org/wiki/Capitalism

Wikipedia. (2016, June 27). *Civil forfeiture in the United States.* Retrieved from Wikipedia: https://en.wikipedia.org/wiki/Civil_forfeiture_in_the_United_States

Memorandum to the African Americans

Wikipedia. (2016, June 20). *History of capitalism.* Retrieved from Wikipedia:
   https://en.wikipedia.org/wiki/History_of_capitalism

Wikipedia. (2016, June 27). *Tulsa race riot.* Retrieved from Wikipedia:
   https://en.wikipedia.org/wiki/Tulsa_race_riot

World Socialist Movement. (2016, June 26). *What is Capitalism?* Retrieved from World
   Socialist Movement: http://www.worldsocialism.org/english/what-capitalism

Memorandum to the African Americans

Mission Statement

The mission of the African American Organization is to unite Twenty- five million African Americans on an economic level, as never before in our history. Our purpose is to carry out capitalistic endeavors through our membership. In order to bring about a positive economic change, in the African American communities and experiences with one another. Our first order of business is to acquire an accumulation and ownership of capital, from and within the membership. This will enable the African American Organization to open training centers, to train members of the African American Organization to control all aspects of the African American Organization businesses in American and Globally.

In this mission, the ultimate goal is to get all members to receive a dividend throughout their lives, where their money is working for them and not them just working for money. Also before of the member's death, the African American Organization will insist that all members make a will and testament, to pass on dividends their receiving to their offspring's or in anyone in their African American family. The purpose of this is for African American children, or the next generation to have an inheritance to continue, the development of wealth and promoting the capitalistic system, started by the African American Organization.

Therefore, we must make African Americans aware of the purchasing and money power we have in our possession, and the need to harness this power, through capitalism and for the posterity of African Americans. The African American Organization has no illusions that this will take an act of God, for the unity of African Americans working together on such a large scale, we stand ready and able to execute this mission.